Finding & Hiring The BEST Childcare

Melissa Martz

Finding and Hiring The BEST Childcare

tellwell

Tellwell Talent
www.tellwell.ca

ISBN
978-1-77302-298-7 (Paperback)
978-1-77302-297-0 (eBook)

Praise for "Inclusive Playgrounds: Play for Every Child"

"Inclusive Playgrounds is an organized, well-thought-out, invaluable guide for those who understand the vital importance of inclusive play, but don't know where to start. Author Melissa Martz has combined compelling personal anecdotes with detailed, practical information to set community groups on the right course."

—LISA BENDALL
Freelance Writer, Author

" Surely this should be part of the syllabus for students entering the field."

—PETER ETRIL SNYDER
Artist

"Inclusive Playgrounds: Play for Every Child is an interesting, informative and valuable resource for parents, educators and politicians who want to ensure all children, regardless of mobility, have accessible playgrounds."

—DAVID C. ONLEY
28th Lieutenant- Governor of Ontario

"I learned so much reading this book!

As a busy parent of six kids, one on the autism spectrum. I had not even considered some of the many issues regarding accessibility and play spaces. An important read for parents and educators."

—JULIE COLE
Co-Founder of Mabels Labels

TABLE OF CONTENTS

PREFACE

In November 1997, I began my career as a full-time, live-out Nanny. Now 19 years later I still hold this title, and loving every minute of it.

Within these years, I can't tell you how many times I have been questioned about childcare options, questions to ask potential childcare providers, oh....and if I could become their Nanny. Sorry folks, I am a long term Nanny, I stay until the family doesn't need me anymore; I don't leave beforehand.

When I started writing this book and told people what it would be about, I received comments like *"Yes! Every parent goes through this – it's totally relevant!", "childcare is certainly an interesting topic and a challenging one for parents returning to work."* With that validation, made me more excited to get this book out, a simple, concise, and straightforward guide to acquire the best childcare arrangement for your family.

In 2012 I wrote an article that I pitched to *ParentsCanada* about hiring a Nanny, and it was quickly responded with something like "Yes...we'd love an article like this!" After that article was published (yes, you get to read that article on the next page), continuously being asked about finding childcare, and noticing there were no books solely on this subject, I knew I had to write one!

The different types of childcare are explored, complete with the pro's and con's for each kind. The chapter on hiring childcare gives you a thorough guide on where to find, and how to find each childcare option. On the flip side, you could find yourself needing to fire your childcare provider; I've covered that topic too. I have interwoven my experiences all throughout the pages of this book.

Every child deserves the best childcare possible, I trust this book will help to achieve that goal. After all, finding childcare is one of the most important decisions you will have to make if you are a working parent.

It all started with this article...

HOW TO LAND YOUR MARY POPPINS

Original publication date: June, 2012 issue of ParentsCanada

By: Melissa Martz

Original publication for *ParentsCanada* Magazine: May/June 2012

You've probably watched the 1964 Disney classic many times. Now that your family needs a Nanny, you may well wonder if there is a Mary Poppins in your future.

In my years as a nanny, I have had good and bad experiences. The negative ones were the result for my profession being misunderstood. A good experience begins with a clear understanding of what services a nanny can, and should deliver.

A nanny is not a babysitter. Nor is she a maid or housekeeper.

She is responsible for the safe and nurturing care of your children. One family's expectations of a nanny's responsibilities may be entirely different from the next, so be sure to state your expectations up front.

But first you need to figure out what kind of nanny you're looking for: Live-in or live-out.

LIVE-IN NANNY

Live-in nannies earn about $400-$500 every two weeks, depending on where you live, with money deducted for room and board.

They become a part of your family, sharing in many of your activities. Many families choose to hire a live-in caregiver from abroad who want to work in Canada. Citizen and Immigration Canada (CIC) will issue a work permit for a person who has a job offer from a Canadian sponsor to be eligible to hire a nanny from abroad, an employer must apply for an receive a positive Labour Market Opinion from ServiceCanada. A live-in caregiver must work for you in a private home on a full-time basis, live with you, and have a private, furnished room within your home. You must pay for her health insurance enrol her in provincial workplace safety insurance (also known as workers' compensation), and pay for her travel costs to get her from her country to Canada. (For more on the Live-in Caregiver Program visit cic.gc.ca.)

This was the choice for Sandra Bratty, a mother of four from Kettleby, Ont. She began her search in January, 2011 and didn't connect with her candidate until September. The process is tedious and involves lots of paperwork, along with security and immigration approvals.

Nanny Robina, the resident nanny on The Mom Show on Slice TV says "I was a live-in nanny with many families for almost 30 years and, in my experience, you really become a part of the family. When hiring a nanny from overseas, however, take into consideration what culture she comes from. She may come from a country that has a lifestyle quite different from Canadian culture."

On the other hand, exposure to a different culture is often a plus of hiring a nanny from another country.

Calgary mom, Jill Drader worked as a nanny (or au pair) during her university years. Now she employs nannies from France to care for her son, Jake. "An au pair in Europe is the logical choice for our family," she says. "In our neighbourhood, there are babysitters and daycare centres, but the centres close at 6 p.m. And I'm not always home from work by that time. An au pair was the answer for us because it has provided safety and security by having someone who has become part of the family. My son is comfortable with her and she knows our routines and lifestyle."

THE LIVE-OUT NANNY

The wage for a live-out nanny can vary between $10.25 to $18 an hour, depending on the nanny's experience, qualifications, and where you live. If you are looking for help for, say $50 a day, then a nanny may not be in your budget.

Live out nannies arrive at a designated time in the morning, and leave at a specific time at the end of the day. Nanny Robina notes that live-out nannies are interestingly hard to find. Further, you have to cope with their bus being late or their car being stuck in the snow.

THE SEARCH

Unfortunately, your nanny won't float down from the sky with suitcase and umbrella in hand.

She may arrive, however, by way of a great recommendation from a family or friend. Nanny Robina agrees the happiest relationships come from word-of-mouth recommendations.

Ironically, my current family lives on the same street where, in the initial interview, we both knew some of the neighbours. This was a great start for both of us!

Besides word-of-mouth, here are some surefire ways to start building your list of candidates:

*Visit www.canadiannanny.ca This lists nannies across Canada, along with their profiles.

*Ask for referrals from other nannies, especially those in happy situations.

*Check out an agency. "I have always gone through agencies because of their screening process and security," says Sandra. The agency Nanniesoncall.ca is the best one I have experienced."

Beware of agencies that don't always have nannies available or who place nannies who are inexperienced.

Agencies interview and screen potential candidates and then put them on a database. Families are then given a list of matches that best suit their needs. Most agencies charge a one-time fee of 10 percent of the nanny's annual gross income.

THE INTERVIEW

Prepare your questions. This is a time for full disclosure on both sides as to expectations. Ask...

-Why did you apply for this position?

-What is your past experience? (Ask for references)

-Describe any difficult problem in the past and how did you handle it?

-How do you handle aggressive behaviour between children?

-How do you handle children who refuse to eat?

-How would you handle someone at the door who claims to be a relative and wants entry?

-How do you handle children who cry endlessly and are inconsolable?

-Will you contribute to keeping the house tidy? What chores will do do or not do?

THE QUALIFICATIONS

Check the specifics. Does she have training in first aid, CPR, early childhood education or child development?

And then the intangibles. Does she seem responsible, mature and, maybe most important, does she have a sense of humour?

THE DECISION

Trust your instincts and first impressions as to whether the nanny is a fit for your family. When you reach an agreement on expectations and duties, the days and hours of work, wages, overtime pay, and vacation time put all in a contract. This is for the protection of both you and your nanny. Have an accountant or financial advisor set up a business number, too. You are legally required to remit payroll deductions for taxes, EI, and CPP on your nanny's behalf.

CHAPTER ONE

Pros and Cons of Childcare Options

CHILDCARE OPTIONS GALORE

Alright, so you will need childcare for your child(ren) once you return to work. Great! What type? Are you wanting family or friends to care for your children, a daycare centre, home based childcare provider, a nanny? Depending on what kind of childcare you are looking at will determine when you seriously begin looking at your options. Did you notice I didn't include the word 'babysitter'? When I think of babysitter, I think of the series of books by Ann M. Martin, I think of teenagers babysitting on weekends, grandparents/other family members caring for the children for a few hours here and there. Whenever someone refers me as a babysitter, I quickly correct them saying I am a nanny. *"But it's the same thing"* they argue. You might think it is, but it really is not.

If you are wanting a spot at a daycare centre, you will need to register on OneList, a comprehensive list of licensed daycare centres, licensed home based childcare, before/after school care at schools, and nursery/pre-schools. And, because daycare spots seem to be difficult to get, it is suggested you register your name on the list as soon as you make the choice you want a licensed daycare for your child; even when you are still pregnant.

Siobhan, at only two months pregnant already knew what kind of childcare she would per sue for her son/daughter. After maternity leave, she will put them in the daycare at the university she attends.

FAMILY/FRIENDS

I know several families who rely on grandparents or other family members or friends to care for their children on a daily basis while they are at work. The reasons for deciding upon the family route for your childcare needs can be from a financial standpoint, cultural (many Portuguese and Italian grandparents care for their grandchildren when parents are working) to spending time with and developing a great relationship with the grandparents.

Although, all these reasons are all fine and good, I personally don't agree with having grandparents being the full-time childcare providers (or Babysitters....there, I said it.) I mean, it's OK for a day or two a week, after all that is one of the job requirements grandparents are bestowed. I feel the same way using other family members or friends as the full-time childcare situation. Yes, there are emergency situations or childcare provider's holidays when the need for grandparent's caregiving skills are needed. Even if you live with the grandparents (or they live with you) they should not be expected to all of a sudden be full-time childcare providers.

Don't get me wrong, I am not telling you not to have this arrangement, that it won't work. I know of families who have been the full-time daycare providers, and it has been a positive experience all around. I'm just saying you don't want anything to happen to your relationship with the family member or friend if this arrangement goes sour.

You don't want to personally let go of *your* personal beliefs of raising children to your family member's beliefs, especially if they are with your children day in, day out. After all, you might be getting free childcare, so they might think they are entitled. Take advice, yes, but if the way they are doing things (and I'm not talking about the act of spoiling them here and again....again, a grandparent's prerogative) but their whole child-rearing philosophy might not coincide with yours.

Having said this, having grandparents as your day-to-day daycare can work, and I know of many that do, just make sure you clearly lay out your expectations (i.e. Spoiling rules...different when grandparents see them less frequently than five days a week) you might consider registering for different programs for them to do together, for example: library programs, swimming, art programs, music programs, or even consider putting them in a preschool a few mornings a week to break up their day, and your child has interaction with other children.

PROS AND CONS OF FAMILY CHILDCARE

Pros

-Financially-friendly

-You feel secure that it's another family member looking after your children.

-When your child is sick, they are most likely still cared for by the family member.

-Grandparent/Grandchildren spend quality time together

-Flexibility

Cons

-It ties grandparents down...you don't want them to get tired of caring for their grandchildren day in/day out.

-social outings and interaction with other children might be sparse or obsolete

-Next to no structure in the day....if that is what you are wanting.

-Too much TV time might happen.

Good caregivers are gold. If you've managed to find a {childcare provider} who is reliable, compassionate, and can handle your half-pint, do what you can to make sure she sticks around. Treat her with kindness. Remember her with small gifts or cards on special occasions. Offer her flexibility when she needs it. Don't skimp on her salary and say thank you – no one gets tired of hearing it!

-Taken from "Raising a Kid with Special Needs" by Lisa Bendall
Used with permission.

DAYCARE CENTRES

Did you know that The Day Nurseries Act was produced in 1946, a lengthy document that defines childcare in Ontario, and how childcare should be provided? Only, in 1946 a vast majority of women stayed home to raise their families, so there was no need for such thing as a daycare centre. Children stayed home until they were old enough for school.

The outdated and long overdue updated version of that document took effect on August 31, 2015. It is now referred to as the Childcare and Early Years Act. This act applies to licensed daycare centres, licensed home childcare, nursery/preschools, and before and after school programs in elementary schools.

I won't go into detail about the document itself, as it is a long, drawn out outline, thoroughly dictating all areas of a day at a licensed daycare centre.

According to the YWCA Canada study "Educated, Employed, and Equal: the Economic Prosperity Case for National Child Care" (2011), 66.5 per cent of Canadian mothers with children under the age of five belong to the paid labour market, but there only licensed childcare spaces for approximately one in five Canadian children under the age of 5 (Early Childhood Education and Care in Canada Childcare Resource and Research Unit, 2008).

To be honest, I am not a huge fan of daycare centres. I find they are too structured, too 'school-like' for my liking when children are so young. Daycare centres are a breathing ground for germs and illness.

If you are wanting a spot at a daycare centre (only approximately 20% of spots are licensed), you will need to register on OneList, a comprehensive list of licensed daycare centres, licensed home based childcare, before/after school care at schools, and nursery/pre-schools. And, because daycare spots seem to be difficult to get, it is suggested you register your name on the list as soon as you make the choice you want a licensed daycare for your child; even when you are still pregnant. When you visit individual websites of the daycare centres you might be interested in, you will most likely notice at the bottom of the page that you read that you are required to register on OneList. As of September 2016, the wait list fees have been lifted in Ontario for licensed daycare centres and licensed home child-care agencies.

Registering on OneList alleviates you from contacting every daycare centre in the phonebook to ask if there are available spots for your intended date of returning to work (this is what use to happen) or if you need to be put on wait lists. It's quick and easy to register and you can enter all the locations of centres/home based childcare in one click. Childcare subsidy and support for children with disabilities can be applied here as well. When a spot becomes available in your desired locations, you are supposed to be notified to see if you are still wanting a spot at that particular centre. If OneList works in your favour of where and when you need daycare, then consider yourself one of the lucky ones; it doesn't seem to happen too often. OneList or OneHSN (Human Services Network) are available in a majority of the communities in Ontario including: Waterloo Region, Brantford, Niagara, London, Bruce County, Thunder Bay, Ottawa, Lambton.

Ula put her name on OneList in November 2014 for a spot at a preschool for her 2.5 year old daughter. She received a call in January 2015, but because they were on vacation, they had to give up the spot to another person, but then they received another call in May saying there was an available spot at that same preschool. Ula was one of the lucky ones.

Personally, I have heard a lot of negativity from parents trying to use OneList to find a daycare centre for their child. Ula's experience was the ONLY positive one I heard.

Leanne registered with OneList when her daughter was one year old wanting one of two childcare centres close to her home. Her daughter is now three years old, and still she has no spot.

In the case of OneList, you need to, as David on W Network ' *Love It or List It'*, says, broaden your search and go outside of your neighbourhood for a hopeful, guaranteed spot at a childcare centre the date of your return to work.

Cameron and Jenny registered when she was five months pregnant with their first child in hopes there would be a daycare spot when Jenny goes back to work January 2017. Their daughter is now four months old (April 2016) and they don't feel confident a spot will be available.

Tiffany use to be the registrar at a parent co-operative preschool who would contact people from the OneList database that a spot in the pre-school was available. But, she said that interestingly, clients who applied via OneList complained that centres were not contacting them. *"We, (and other centres as well) found that families were not responding to our responses to their applications."* Tiffany came to the conclusion that perhaps people were entering their emails incorrectly or applying to a gazillion places and not responding to the ones that weren't their first choice. It was very frustrating for everyone. The moral of the story: register at your own risk. When you do register with OneList, have a backup childcare arrangement in mind just in case the OneList database doesn't work out in your favour. Be on alert for centres responding to your request even if they were not your first choice. After all, you entered that particular centre as one of your choices in the first place. You can always choose to leave that facility if another more convenient location becomes available.

PROS AND CONS OF DAYCARE CENTRES

Pros

-convenient locations

-licensed

-Half day/full day programs

-structured programs

-socialization

-Tax write-off

-educated, experienced staff

-a whole range of experiences are available for your child, they otherwise might not get

-children with special needs are included

Cons

-long wait lists

-expensive if you have more than one child

-inconvenient if you are running late....it'll cost you!

-breathing ground for germs....kids get sick quite often

-many don't take the ages when you need it (i.e. maternity leave ends when your baby is 12 months old, but you have to wait until your baby is 18 months old.)

Cost

At daycare centres, there are different fees for care for different age groups: infants, toddlers, preschoolers, school-aged. Daycare centres are relatively have the same price range; there might be a difference of $10 or so. This is why you have to do your homework beforehand for what you will be expected to pay, so there are no surprises when your 'number' comes up at a daycare centre, and your child is offered a spot at the centre. You can certainly decline but wouldn't it sound embarrassing to do so because you didn't check out the price vs. another choice that you let slip through your fingers because you didn't do your homework.

Dollars and cents count....make it count.

Here are a few examples of what you would be expected to pay at Early Learning Childcare Centres:

YMCA

Full Day

Infant	$72.50
Toddler	$54.00
Pre-school	$46.00

Half Day

No half-day option for infants

Toddler	$36.50
Pre-school	$33.50

Nursery School

Toddler	$30.00
Preschool	$27.00

Before/After School

JK-Grade 6	$44.25 (full-day)
	$9.80 (Before)
	$14.70 (After)

Bright Starts

Full-time

Infants	$1,150.00/month	$69.89/daily

Toddlers	$1,160.00/month	$53.33/daily

Part-time

No option for part-time care for infants

Toddler	$545/month	(2 days)
	$785/month	(3 days)
Preschool	$935/month	
Camp:	$230/week	

Milton's Kids and Company

Full time

Infants	$1,490.00
Toddlers	$1,310.00
Preschool	$1,190.00

As you can see, daycare centres can get quite costly, especially if you have more than one child.

Recently I was asked about how much it would cost to hire a Nanny vs sending three children to a daycare centre; that is twin 1 yr olds, and a preschooler. I used one of the examples of what you would pay at a daycare centre to calculate what this family would be paying each week for two infants and a preschooler: 2 infants (before 18 months) $72.50 = $144.00 per day, plus $46.50 per day for a preschooler. Grand total for a week's worth of childcare at a daycare centre: $950.00 (or thereabouts as each centre is not exactly the same). I said quickly "go with a Nanny!.... here is my article in ParentsCanada on finding a Nanny....and register on www.canadiannanny.ca"

A Little More [Erick Traplin]

Could I please have a hug, could I please have a
kiss, could I please have a little more
and would you please tie my shoe, and would you please open the door
it's time to go outside and play, it's time to greet the day
could I please have a hug, could I please have a kiss
and I'll be on my way
I'm gonna take my car, I'm gonna take my truck
I'm gonna take my aeroplane
my friends and I we'll share our toys, and play a little game
chorus
I'm gonna take my ball, I'm gonna take my doll
I'm gonna take all of my blocks
we'll take turns playing with them, in the big sandbox
chorus
1,2,3,4,5,6,7, you know I love you
1,2,3,4,5,6,7 and you love me too
so if you have the time
and if you don't mind
could I ask this of you
could I please have a hug, could I please have a kiss
could I please have a little more
could I please have a hug, could I please have a kiss
could I please have a little more

HOME DAYCARE

Isn't it interesting when you put a poll question on a social media outlet like Facebook ~ almost immediately you are bombarded with responses. That is exactly what happened when I posted the question *'Who either went to a home childcare provider as a child, or send their children to a home childcare provider now?'* I received approximately 75 replies. Then, in the Facebook group 'KWC Childcare Providers and Parents Connect' brought another 74 names, while several names popped into mind as I did this. The locations of home childcare providers in most any city in Canada, surpass the number of coffee shops in the city.

The verdict? Home childcare providers are the single most used child-care arrangement, more so daycare centres and nannies (I have kleenex beside me:)

The home childcare setting appeals to parents because of a home/family atmosphere during the day when they are at work ~ if parents are unable to be in their own home when you go to work, they can, at their second home – and it is a home.

Home childcare providers are for the most part, stay-at-home parents who want to be home for their own children, but also bring in an income.

Unlike daycare centres which are all licensed, there are both licensed and unlicensed home childcare providers. A break-down of licensed and unlicensed childcare providers are below. Basically the same rules apply to both. For one, home childcare provider, whether they are licensed or not, can only care for care for five children at any one given time, including their own children. The new guidelines that came into effect on September 1, 2015 of how many of each age of children home childcare providers are allowed to care for at any one given time are in effect for all home childcare providers, across the board. A childcare provider, licensed or unlicensed can only care for two children under the age of two, three children under the age of three, and five children under the age of five. This count includes any of their own children under the age of five. I know of home childcare providers who have five children full time, who bring in a nice paycheque.

If you have twins, a home daycare potentially could be the best childcare choice for you providing the provider you have in mind has room for both of your 1 year olds...remember only two children under two is mandated across the home childcare board in Ontario. Did someone say nanny? A nanny will be your best choice, as you will see in the coming pages.

Cost

The cost of sending your child(ren) to a home daycare provider can vary between $35-$50 a day, depending on the provider. Each home daycare provider is different for what they charge per day. I hear grumbling from parents all the time of how much childcare costs, and I just roll my eyes. Yes, it is an expense, but it is an expense that multiplies in benefits every day with seeing your child happy, learning to be social and thriving. You can't put a price on that. Putting money into your childcare arrangement will be money well spent. I often give the example of a parent who on one hand grumbles that childcare arrangement is simply too expensive, and then they turn around and buy a brand new $40,000 vehicle.

I recall a lady from a preschool I helped out at for a few years asked me if I could look after her daughter for the afternoon. Now, keep in mind this lady was very well to do: I told her my fee, and she said "*oh, I would never pay that for childcare*"....then in her next breath, I overheard her say to someone that she paid $500 for Botox injections. Hmmm....

LICENSED DAYCARE PROVIDERS

Being a licensed daycare provider simply means the childcare provider works for an agency (i.e. Region of Waterloo – one of the only regional home childcare programs in the province), or an agency like Wee Watch. The agency checks in with their home childcare providers, supervising them with home visits and updates, making sure that the care they are providing is at the highest standard.

Licensed daycare providers are not licensed by the Ministry of Education, but rather the agency they work for.

Wee Watch was started in 1984, providing licensed home daycare across Ontario. To date, there are 85 locations. They follow the same guidelines as the Region. One thing about WeeWatch is, you do not have to go through OneList. You only need to download an application, and wait to be matched with a provider. Wee Watch providers receive:

-monthly home visits

-quarterly home safety checks

-annual area supervisor visits

And you receive:

-a summary report from your provider

-monthly summary sheets

-calendar of programs and meal plans are posted

-back-up service for days when your provide
is off due to illness or holidays.

Not only does one need a criminal reference check in the vulnerable sector to become a licensed childcare provider, but every adult who resides at that address needs to complete criminal records check before care can go forward.

Licensed childcare providers are given a binder of resources, policies and procedures to follow.

The agency the childcare provider works for finds families for her, and introduces them to see if they are a good match.

The agency regularly pays the provider; the families do not pay the provider themselves.

In August 2015, there were 1,715 spaces available for licensed Region home daycare. The projected amount that a family would have to pay for a 3 year old to attend licensed home daycare by the Region was between $9,750.00-$11,500.00.

Subsidy

Did you know that 80% of families who receive a childcare subsidy are single parents? The other 20% are 2 parent families. Approximately 52% of these families receive a net income of $20,000 or less.

The reasons why one would need a childcare subsidy are varied:

Working – 66%

School – 19%

Special needs/Social needs: 11%

Other (i.e Medical, Seeking Employment) - 3%

UNLICENSED CHILDCARE PROVIDERS

The majority of childcare providers I have met along the way in my career as a Nanny have been unlicensed, although a few have been licensed.

Unlicensed childcare providers seek out their own families, meaning they have to advertise themselves, get recommendations from other families.

With unlicensed childcare providers, the family is responsible for the supervision, and ensuring the care of their children are of the highest standard, no agency does that for them.

Both going the licensed provider or unlicensed provider route has its merits and pitfalls. It boils down to if you want to work through an agency and allow them to handle finding a match for you, supervision, payment, or if you want to do all of that yourself.

New Rules for Unlicensed Providers January 1, 2016

1. Daycare providers must count their own children under the age of six

2. Daycare providers can only care for a maximum two children under the age of 2.

Come *August 31, 2017* Daycare providers must include 10,11 and 12 yr olds in the total of children they care for their own 10, 11 or 12 year old are counted in this total.

Follow the Rules or Else:

If a provider has more than the permitted number of children in her care, a penalty starting at $2,000 per child/per day is charged.

If a providers own 4 or 5 year old attending full-day kindergarten or grade 1, they only need to count them in the 5 children during the summer. They don't need to be included in their count during the school year (including March Break and PA Days) as long as:

-care is between 6:00 am-7:00 pm

-the provider cares for a max of one child younger than 2 years of age

-the provider has not been convicted under the DNA (Day Nurseries Act) or OCEYA (Ontario Child Early Years Association)

Pros and Cons of Home Daycares

Pros

-convenient locations

-cost-efficient, especially when you have more than one child

-socialization

-tax write-off

-routine with daily schedule of activities

-home/family environment

-in a licensed home daycare, all adults are required to have police checks done

LICENSED DAYCARE PROVIDERS

-meet health and safety standards

-government regulated and inspected

-provides caregiver professional development, support and monitoring

-child-care fee subsidies available

-once per year the Ministry of Education may inspect home daycare provider locations that are under a home daycare agency.

Cons

-inconvenient pick-up times if you work late

-if childcare provider is sick or on holidays, parents need to find alternate childcare arrangements

-you may not be guaranteed a spot(s) if you go on maternity leave with the same provider. ***I do recall one lady who kept paying the home daycare the full year she was on maternity leave, so she wouldn't lose a spot. I know that is often financially impossible, but in some cases, that could be done.*

-conflict with other families if problems arise between children.

Cost

At daycare centres, there are different fees for care for different age groups: infants, toddlers, preschoolers, school-aged. Daycare centres are relatively have the same price range; there might be a difference of $10 or so. This is why you have to do your homework beforehand for what you will be expected to pay, so there are no surprises when your 'number' comes up at a daycare centre, and your child is offered a spot at the centre. You can certainly decline but wouldn't it sound embarrassing to do so because you didn't check out the price vs another choice that you let slip through your fingers because you didn't do your homework.

NANNY

Babysitter vs. Nanny: The Difference

So you, or someone you know thinks a babysitter and a nanny are one in the same. Allow me to be the one to differentiate the two for you...

Babysitter:

A babysitter simply provides custodial care, meaning keeping a child safe and entertained for a few short hours on an as-needed basis (i.e. date nights). This care is often used on weekends, weeknights, or after school. They are often high school or college/university students for these occasions, but of course grandparents fit this bill as well.

Yes, I use to be a night time babysitter....in high school!

Nanny:

First off, being a Nanny is a REAL job.

In November 1997, I became a full-time, long-term Nanny. I stay with a family as long as they need me. I work approximately 40 hours a week. The longest period I was a full-time Nanny was five years, the shortest was 10 months. I am fully invested in the child's development and well-being, and an integral part of each of these families lives while employed by them. I essentially help raise their children; the activities and programs I put in our day each week mirrors this investment in the development of the whole child. ****I'll detail the different activities my 'kids' and I have partaken in in the chapter on Hiring a Nanny.* Some people think that if you have a Nanny, the children are at home all day, with no social interaction. I'm here to tell you that is completely the opposite: a good Nanny will seek out social interaction opportunities in a variety of different settings. There are both Live-in and Live-out Nannies. I've always been a Live-out Nanny. This means I come at at a specific time each morning, and work until a specific time each night. Live-in is just that, they live in their employer's home. A room (or in some cases more) is provided for them as their personal quarters. Live-in Nannies have a pre-determined work schedule of the hours of work where they are 'on duty'.

PROS AND CONS OF NANNIES:

Pros

-child doesn't have to get up super early to get to the childcare arrangement. (When I come, Lauren is still in her jammies, having breakfast)

-1:1 attention

-long-term

-flexible

-if a child is sick, a Nanny still comes to care for the child (unlike daycare centres or home daycares)

*less expensive if you have more than one child in care

*tax write-off

Cons

-hiring a Nanny can be expensive

-child might be alone a lot if Nanny isn't involving child in programs and events for social interaction

-if the Nanny is sick, you need to find other arrangements for childcare

-if you have a live-in Nanny from another country, you might go through several before your child goes to school

-you might lose your Nanny if you go on maternity leave, and have to let her go because you are financially unable to keep her for the time you are off work.

COST

Hiring a nanny can be expensive for a family, but when I think about the amount families at daycare centres, I don't know what all the fuss is about. The hourly wage for a live-out nanny can be anywhere between $13-$18. There are various factors to consider when determining the salary of a nanny:

-years of experience and/or education

-expected duties of the nanny (ie if maintaining the home includes grocery shopping, other errands, laundry, cooking, cleaning).

You're My Angel [**Erick Traplin**]

Give Me One Hug, And I'll Give You Two
Give Me One Kiss And I'll Give You Three
For You Are The Sweetest Kid Around
You Never Ever Walk Around With A Frown
You Always Have A Smile For Everyone
You're My Angel, You're My Angel
Give Me Two Hugs And I'll Give You Three
Give My Two Kisses And I'll Give You Four (Do You Want More?)
You Run Around The House Looking For Hiding Places
Then You Jump Out Making Silly Faces
You Make Me Laugh So Much My Heart Races (Embraces)
You're My Angel, You're My Angel
And When I Feel A Little Sad
I Watch You Play And It's Not So Bad
You're My Angel
Give Me Three Hugs And I'll Give You Four
Give Me Three Kisses And I'll Give You More
You're Up In The Morning With The Rising Sun
You're Busy All Day Just Having Fun
You Only Slow Down When The Day Is Done
You're My Angel, You're My Angel
And When I Feel A Little Sad
I Look At You And It's Not So Bad
You're My Angel
Give Me One Hug And I'lll Give You Two
Spoken... Nighty Night My Little Angel

CHAPTER 2

Hiring Childcare

HIRING CHILDCARE

Now that you've learned a little bit about what each type of childcare is about, you may have already contemplated what type of childcare you want to pursue for your family. I know, it's a very important, daunting and time consuming task to ensure you are making the very best decision. Let me help you with a more detailed description of how you hire childcare, the best places to find the childcare arrangement that suits your family, questions to ask, what to look for in a candidate.

Here are some general topics that more or less relate to the three childcare avenues we're talking about.

NEVER TOO EARLY TO SEARCH FOR CHILDCARE

But first, let me start out by saying it is not too early to start your search (even if you, your spouse or your Aunt Phyllis think it's too early). You might think you have all the time in the world, after all, you'll be off for a year, that's plenty of time, right? Well, it depends...do you want to find the best of the best? Can you ever be too late? Yes, you can. If you wait too long, begin to scramble for childcare, you might not be thinking clearly of what you really want in a childcare provider, and you take the first person that comes your way, no matter if you actually like them or not. You just need someone to watch your kids because you begin work in two days. It's my hope that you haven't done that, or know people who have. Yes, there are instances when all of a sudden you have a new job starting next week, but for the most part, you have ample time to find care (especially if you are on a 12 month or more maternity leave).

Having said that, my position as a Nanny has had fluctuating times when I've been hired, and when I actually started work. The shortest was less than a week: my first employer, whom I had cared for her children in the evening for several years, called to say she was taking Lauren (the first of my four Lauren's, thus far) out of the daycare centre she went to, because she was called from work to come pick her up for the umpteenth time because she was sick with what it seemed, another ear infection. Jenny decided right then and there she was pulling her out of the daycare centre. It was a short time after this occurred when Jenny phoned me and asked if I could be Lauren's full-time Nanny. That was one week (actually evening of when I had my wisdom teeth out and she was surprised at how well I was speaking) and I started the following Monday. Lauren never had another ear infection again.

A former classmate of mine and I walked past each other at our neighbourhood shopping mall when her daughter Emma was a mere 3 weeks old, exchanged pleasantries and went off on our merry way. The way Kelly tells it is that she looked back at me and wondered *"I wonder if Melissa babysits."* (I know THAT WORD.) I've spoken to Kelly about that:) Kelly went home and asked her Aunt (who once was married to my Uncle....and because of that we share three cousins...but I'll leave that story for the book *Who are the People in your Family.* Just visualize Bob from Sesame Street singing the tune. Our Aunt wasn't too sure, but she thought so. I found out about Kelly wanting to explore the possibility of me being Emma's Nanny from one of our cousins, at of all places, my grandmother's funeral. The connection was made, and when Emma was 3 months old, I was hired to be her Nanny to start the next calendar year, when she was 10 months old. This is a fine example of not waiting to the last minute to find the care you desire for your child. Many amazing connections were made because of this particular job, and for that, I will forever be grateful to Kelly.

Bubbles (Erick Traplin)

There's bubbles, bubbles, bubbles in the air
bubbles, bubbles, bubbles
everywhere
There's bubbles on the chair, there's bubbles in my hair
Bubbles, bubbles, bubbles everywhere
I like blowin' bubbles, I blow them one by one
A little soap and water and the fun has just begun
I blow them in the air, I blow them on my toes
And when I'm feelin' silly, I blow them out my nose
I pop them with my hands, I pop them with my feet
I pop them in my mouth, they taste kind of sweet
I chase them all around the yard as they go spinning by
If I could I'd chase them, right up into the sky
I like watching bubbles as they're floating through the air,
When the sun shines on them there's rainbows everywhere
They dance upon a summer breeze and up into the sky
Without a worry, or a care, or a reason why

DON'T WAIT...IT MIGHT BE TOO LATE

Before I had my first Nanny position in 1997, I had been asked by my cousin who was pregnant at the time, and ran a home daycare about me working for her for a few months after she had her first child. I never heard back from her, and then a few months later was asked to be a full-time Nanny to a 16 month old. I recall her saying that it was her fault, for not talking to me sooner about the position.

When I was looking for my current position, I actually had interviews with four families in the same week! Each interview was pretty good, and I understood that my references were going to be checked. I then received an email from Catherine, who really wanted to meet me to talk about me being her daughter Lauren, 9 months, full-time Nanny. I replied saying that I had a family that was very interested, and were in the process of checking my references, so to be fair, I had to wait for them. Catherine understood and respected this. Then, when I was with two of my former kids, Emma and Lauren at an Erick Traplin concert (you see his songs dispersed throughout this book), I asked one of my references if they had been contacted about me yet, and they said No. I then received a phone call just before the concert started from that family saying they were going to go another route for childcare. After the concert, when the girls were busy talking with Erick, I checked my email, and there was yet another email from Catherine, sounding desperate *"I know you are waiting for other people to get back to you...but can we just meet?"* I replied *"Yes! Let's meet. Tomorrow good?"* Unbeknownst to me until I got home to see Catherine's reply; she lived a mere twenty steps from the library location I had just been at. Is that serendipity or what?

WORKING 9-5 IS NOT EVERYONE'S WAY TO MAKE A LIVING

Oh sorry, do you have the song rolling in your head now? I didn't mean to do that, honest! :)

Not everyone who needs daycare has a 9-5 job, so that might limit your choices for daycare. A majority of daycare centres open at 6:00 am and close at 6:00 pm. But, if you work out of town, and get stuck in traffic, and

Richmond Public Library - Brighouse
100 - 7700 Minoru Gate
Richmond, B.C. V6Y 1R8
604-231-6404
http://www.yourlibrary.ca

Check-out Receipt

May 1, 2024

Checked out to 21290007412929

Title	Finding & hiring the best childcare
Barcode	31290096660824
Due	**05-22-24**

Title	Berlitz Jr. Spanish dictionary /
Barcode	31290006147326
Due	**05-22-24**

miss closing time, you'll pay big time every minute you are late. I've noticed a growing number of home daycare providers who are extending their hours, or make overnight care an option. Your profession can ultimately dictate what avenue of childcare you choose. Do you recall what Jill Drader said at the beginning of this book? No, no, don't go back, you might lose your page! Here it is again: *"In our neighbourhood, there are babysitters and daycare centres, but the centres close at 6 p.m. And I'm not always home from work by that time. An au pair was the answer for us because it has provided safety and security by having someone who has become part of the family. "*

Jobs That 9-5 Doesn't Work:

-Medical Personnel like Hospital Doctors, Nurses, Paramedics

-Police Officers

-Fire Fighters

-You leave early in the morning to travel to a city an hour or so away

-You travel out of province or country for business, and are gone for a few days at a time.

-continental hour shift workers (12 hours)

-You are a musician in the local Symphony (their concerts or rehearsals are all over the place: mornings, afternoons or evenings)

-you work in retail

-you finish work after 6:00 (ie 7:00 or 8:00)

Meghan just returned back to work in television broadcasting after a year's maternity leave with her son. She says *"Childcare is certainly an interesting topic and a challenging one for parents returning to work. We have decided to go with a home daycare based on the fact that I don't finish work until 7:00 pm, and if my husband is travelling, we will need some flexibility with pick-up times."*

It's a good thing that there is not only one daycare arrangement available for everyone. You have many choices here, think about them, weigh the pro's and con's. You'll make the right decision.

Qualifications

I will be the first one not to knock formal College or University ECE education. But, I believe what many new graduates lack is experience. I'm sorry (and I may get hate mail) but I don't agree that the co-op placements are a viable way to say they are *"an experienced ECE professional."* Experience speaks volumes. Yes, the way for graduates to acquire that experience is for daycare centres, schools, or those looking for a nanny to give these graduates a chance. It's just funny when I continuously read ads for ECE graduates that cite *experience preferred* or *experience required.* Now, if you do indeed want someone who is an ECE graduate, may I give you some ideas to think about when looking over their list of qualifications:

a) did they babysit regularly in high school and/or do their co-op placement in a childcare centre or school in high school?

b) were they a camp counsellor, or summer playground leader?

c) did they teach Sunday School or did they lead a church Youth Group

d) are they a Big Brother or Big Sister?

e) are they an SSAH (Special Services at Home Worker) working with a child that has a disability?

f) do they volunteer with an organization that supports children?

I do not have any 'formal' ECE education. I did however take the first of a two year Educational Assistant course, when I believed I was destined to be with my genuine interest in children with special needs. Life has a knack of making things work out, sometimes not the way you originally planned. I started in 1997 as a Nanny, and have never looked back.

Aside from taking a child studies course, I had begun to accumulate being associated (by way of volunteering) with several child related and disability related organizations, my weekend 'babysitting' gigs, taking in seminars and workshops (something I continue to this day), oh yeah...and being the oldest of five children helped groom me into the full-time Nanny I am today.

When I was growing up we had an occasional weekend babysitter, Luanne. Luanne had a genuie love for children. She was a well-known babysitter in the neighbourhood...and beyond. Luanne also lived with Cystic Fibrosis. Luanne has since passed away, but I wanted to write about her, and qualifications to work in childcare for this book, so I emailed her parents to ask permission.

Here is her father's response:

"By all means, you may speak about Luanne in your book! I agree that paper 'qualifications' is not as valid as experience, love, and creativity to care for children. Unfortuantely, some people get a certificate and cannot relate to a door post. They are not screened for their empathy and compassion which are paramount when serving children."

Bear in mind, Luanne's father is a retired high school principal. Pretty amazing response coming from an educator, eh!

Read on...

Because Luanne had Cystic Fibrosis, she knew she would only live for a limited number of years, and she wanted to spend those years doing what she loved to do, caring for children. So, when she was 16 years of age, Luanne quit school and began living her dream job. Luanne cared for multiple families, was asked to be Godmother to one of her charges, and would wok any day of the year....even Christmas Day.

Luanne passed away in 1993. She was 24 years of age.

On June 26, 1994, a neighbourhood playground was dedicated in Luanne's honour.

REFERENCES

Don't be like Mary Poppins, and think providing references are a very old fashioned idea. Well, I'm sorry Mary, but they are not an old fashioned idea. An excellent reference will go a long way.

A WORD ABOUT SPECIAL NEEDS

The one thing that I noticed and commented favourably on the Facebook group 'KWC Childcare Providers and Parents Connect' was that each ad that childcare providers did not put in their ads as "children with special needs are welcome" at all. Children with a disabilities are people first, diagnosis second. Child first language needs to happen; and you, a parent, know that already to speak that way. Depending on your child's personal care needs, you may find childcare at a daycare centre where they have ECE resource teachers to help with 1:1 support or with a nanny who will give them that 1:1 support they need, as they engage with other children in activities at the daycare or in the community.

I agree 100% with inclusion for all children, no matter their ability. But sometimes it's hard for that inclusion to happen at a home daycare, if the care needs are high for one person to attend to when she has say four other children in her care, that need the same top-notch care, with only one adult available to care for them in the house. As Jennifer of Kitchener says *"I don't think it's so much that I would not accept a child with special needs, only that specific needs may not be possible to meet with multiple young children and only one care giver. Certain circumstances can weigh into the ratios as well because some children with specific exceptionalities fall into an under 2 space, even if the age is higher. We cannot take on every child...not for lack of inclusion, but simply for logistics reasons. I appreciate when parents provide information about their children so I can gauge how I can potentially meet those needs for children with special needs I may already be caring for, I want to make sure I can give the kind of care they all deserve too."*

I have often seen ads for an assistant in a home daycare. I now wonder if perhaps there was a child with a disability that required more care than the other children, and having two adults made it possible for them to attend a home daycare.

The child might not be the one with the disability, but the childcare worker. I know of a few individuals who have Down syndrome who work at daycare centres, and I also remember reading a lovely article about someone who has cerebral palsy who worked in the childcare room at a fitness centre.

Three weeks after Kristen, of Vancouver graduated from the ECCE (Early Childhood Care and Education), she was involved in a car accident that left her a Quadriplegic. After taking a few years off for rehab, Kristen started providing story time at her local library, along with subbing for a preschool for a year, and running a music program from babies and toddlers at a recreational centre. Kristen then worked at a daycare centre from 2006-2010. Parents loved that Kristen was a teacher in a wheelchair. The children learned so much: manners (how to treat/talk to person with disabilities), empathy, and developing more responsibility, that helped to foster independence. *"The children were curious as to what happened to me, and I encouraged them to ask questions – a lot of which were geared towards spinal cord injuries."* says Kristen.

Even with me. I have had a stuttering problem all my life. It's a whole lot better than it used to be, but it's still there. All my families know my story (as a young child I was diagnosed with a very mild form of cerebral palsy.... but you would NEVER know it) and it has never been an issue. I did receive some interesting comments from people who had interviewed me in person, or over the phone and I stuttered:

> *"How are toddlers suppose to learn to talk if you stutter?" (yes, someone seriously asked me that, and when I told my most recent employer, could not believe someone would say that.*
>
> *"Do you have seizures or TIA's (mini strokes), is that why you stutter?"*
>
> *"Will you have a conniption if you can't get the words out, and take it out on the children?" (once again, yes, someone seriously asked me that!)*

I don't drive, and it's never been an issue with any of my families. They all loved the fact we took the bus, or walked to our activities. One interesting thing about the family that asked about seizures, and was worried there was some health challenge as to why I didn't drive: the Nanny they ended up hiring came for the Philippines, and she didn't drive. I would see the Nanny (as the next family that interviewed me, hired me) often with the twins (a boy and a girl) often at the same activities I took my next charge, Matthew to. So, what was with the driving issue?

Tanya has provided care for several families over the years. She also has cerebral palsy, but because of how it affects her legs and her gait, she is unable to run. I asked Tanya if any family that she has worked for been concerned that she would not be able to to keep up to the children, and her reply was *"not at all"*.

Along the same thinking I have that every classroom should have a student with a disability, I feel the same way about every childcare arrangement you choose should include a child with a disability (I know, sometimes that's not possible with one adult) the children learn about acceptance, tolerance, similarities/difference. It's true that many children 4 and under have no thoughts about "hey that kid is different"...it sure helps when they are in grade school later on, and they have a classmate that has, for instance, Down syndrome, they most likely will recall their full-time home daycare days, and will have more of an understanding. I am a Nanny for 2 1/2 year old Lauren, one of her best buddies is Desmond. Des has Down syndrome, and is a year and a half older than Lauren. They are teaching each other so much now, and Lauren will, I hope, be able to teach other kids later on in elementary school about children who are "different" and how to be friends, no matter what "disability" they may have.

DON'T PULL ANY PUNCHES

When you are actively looking for childcare, and are in the interviewing stage, please be respectful to all your candidates you interview, and don't lie to them. If you did not choose them as your successful candidate, and state that you have chosen another candidate, but you really didn't. This very thing happened to me. I was interviewed for a nanny position to care for twin 1 year old boys. The next week I was notified and informed that another candidate had been chosen. A few days later I went back on the canadiannanny website, where I had seen their ad in the first place, and they reposted their ad (the date gave it away). I very diplomatically confronted them saying *"I have no problem you choosing another candidate, but when you flat out lie to me, it is not appreciated".*

After all, you don't want your nanny to lie to you, right? (I didn't tell them that.)

Their ad was taken down so fast. No apology, no nothing.

ACCIDENTS HAPPEN

Let's face it: accidents happen.

I recall watching an episode in the 15th season of ER where Dr. Abby Lockhardt fires her son's nanny because he fell at the playground. A little hasty, perhaps. Unfortunately, it's the same scenario that happens all to often – fire the person looking after your children if an accident happens. But, if the same thing happened with the parents close by, then we say "accidents happen".

Example 1: I was looking after a child I often cared for on weekend nights, but this time it was for a week to help kickstart potty training. It was early in the week, I think Tuesday, and I accidentally left the burner on the stove on. That evening I received a phone call to say that my services wouldn't be needed for the rest of the week; even though all was fine. Things happen very unintentionally. Don't rush out and put your HR hat on. Now granted, I was a teenager when this happened, the reaction most likely would have been more of the "that happens" mentality if I were older (which you will see in another example.) ***I apologize to every firefighter family....please don't send me hate mail***

Example 2: Fast forward eight years. I was in the laundry room, putting laundry in the washing machine. During this task, 2 year old Emma was right beside me, and said to me *"Emma is helping"* and I replied *"yes, Emma is such a good helper"* (with my eyes on the laundry). All of a sudden Emma poured a bottle of Duo Action Spray n' Wash on her face (to this day, I have no idea how the heck she opened the bottle right up). Emma's eyes just glazed from that stuff. I sprang into action: I took her upstairs to the change table and started continuously washing her eyes out with water. I then phoned both Telehealth and Poison Control to make sure I was doing the right thing...and I was. Only after all that did I phone Emma's Mom to give her the lowdown on what happened. Later on, Emma did end up gong to Emergency at the hospital just to be checked over. She was fine. I was not reprimanded or fired at all, accidents happen. Granted, if this would have happened early on in my Nanny career, I would have feared I would have been fired. But instead, my employers knew that accidents happen... and it could very well have happened to them.

Example 3: I was at the playground after school with children from two families who nanny-shared me for a year. The playground was full of children and parents. Out of the blue, a boy trips on the playground, and breaks his arm. His mother and grandma took him to the hospital. Just an unfortunate thing that happened. Accidents happen.

Example 4: Just the other day, Lauren and I left to do some errands. We were gone for an hour. When we came home, the front inside door was open. I was almost positive I had slammed the door shut, but apparently not. The first thing I did was call for the dog: she came. I checked to see if the TV was still there, check, my laptop, check. I told my employer what had happened and he laughed when I was mentioning making sure the dog, TV , and laptop were still there...and simply said *"those things happen."*
***I apologize to all police families....yes, I know to alleviate theft, you need to lock the house up. Please don't send me any tickets.**

The same with Accidents Happen....items get lost:

THE LOST MITTEN

One winter's day 21 month old Matthew and I ventured out to the library. When we arrived home, I noticed one of his mitts was missing... it was an expensive brand....I felt terrible!

That evening when I left work, I retraced my steps to the library (in the dark) and found the mitt encased in ice.

My employer's husband was on his way home with the oldest two children from piano lessons, saw me, drove me home, but he thought I had lost my marbles for locating a mitten.

That night, I receive an email citing ***I hereby declare, the award for Nanny of the Year goes to Melissa Martz for going above and beyond the call of duty, and finding missing mitten encased in ice."***

MY MAGIC CARPET

Written By Erick Traplin

I was just a kid when I found my magic carpet
and adventures I had on my magic carpet
I was filled with wonder, I was filled with dreams
I was filled with awe and a thousand scenes
of heroes and heroines and magic and dragons
and little boys and girls with their little red wagons
who won the day
they looked just like me, they looked just like me.

I kept it in my room on a stand beside my bed
and when I took it out I would go wherever it led
I was a pirate, a soldier, a poet, an explorer
in search of excitement that dreams are made of
with heroes and heroines those little boys and girls
who won the day
they look just like me, the look just like me.

I travelled all around the world, on my magic carpet ride
without a care, and wind in my hair
over the world I would go
over deserts and mountains of snow
wherever I wanted to go
adventure awaited, there were worlds to explore
on my magic carpet ride.

I found my magic carpet when I was just a kid
It took me to those places all inside my head
I was filled with wonder, I was filled with dreams
I was filled with awe and a thousand scenes
on every page on every line
and every word was mine all mine
and the heroes and heroines
those little boys and girls
who won the day
they look just like me, they looked just like me
they look just like me, they looked just like me
just like me, just like me, just like me
they looked just like me.

CHAPTER 3

Daycare Centres

As mentioned in the first chapter, back in the day if you wanted your child to attend a specific daycare centre, you would either phone them up or go in and ask if there were any spaces available at that time, and if not, you were put on a waiting list at that specific centre, and they would phone when the availability arose. Now, you are required to put your name on OneList, and what we have seen from the first chapter, it sometimes works, and sometimes doesn't pan out.

Remember reading about Cameron and Jenny in the first chapter? I just received an email from them the other day asking me if I would know any leads to home daycare providers who would have a spot for January 2017 because they have not yet heard anything from OneList, and the prospect of getting a daycare centre looks pretty grim.

OneList Facts:

- Between January 1-August 31, 2015 there were 3,046 new registrants with OneList.
- There is an average of 1,184 new applications per month,.
- There is an average of 380 new children per month.

Here is a three year overview of data at daycare centres in Waterloo Region from 2013-2015.

Number of Early Learning Childcare Centres

- 2013 - 129 centres
- 2014 – 137 centres
- 2015 – 135 centres
- *Number of Spaces*
- 2013 – 4,706
- 2014 – 4,889
- 20155 – 4,844

Percentage of kids (0-4) with access to centre spaces

- 2013 - 17%
- 2014 – 17%
- 2015 – 18%

As you can see there is fluctuation from year to year for various factors:

> *a) families moving into or out of Waterloo Region*
>
> *b) job loss of one or both parents OR the parent who intended to stay home with the children until they were school aged, decided to go back to wok instead to help financially*
>
> *c)family size (having two kids: one boy, one girl, the perfect all-around Canadian family has been thrown out the window)...I have noticed more families opting to increase their family size to three, or more children*
>
> *e) the number of schools offering before and after school care) The new Child Care and Early Years Act that replaces The Day Nurseries Act (previously updated in 1990) was introduced in 2014, and took effect on August 31, 2015 changed the child:age ratio that both daycare centres, and home daycares can have in their care*

To read more about the changes in that have taken effect, read: https://www.ontario.ca/laws/regulation/900262

What to look for in a daycare centre

Awesome! One or more of your choices you entered months ago have a space available for your little one. Now you need to make a decision if that centre you desired a spot in will actually be a good fit for you you and your child.

The first two things you most likely did when listing which daycare centres to put on the OneList registration form were:

> *a) ask for recommendations from friends who have sent their children to that particular daycare centre, an are raving about it*
>
> *OR*
>
> *b) you search (or will now) www.daycarereview.ca The Daycarereview website is a free service for parents to search any childcare facility in Canada; read what others have to say, and what number they rate the centre as. This can be an extremely helpful and calming resource to settle your nerves about going back to work and sending your little one to one their own to foreign territory.*

Ask yourself as you tour your child's prospective daycare centre (without asking any questions):

1. Was I greeted with a smile, and made to feel welcome in the centre?
2. Is the facility clean?
3. Was the centre well staffed? (in Ontario the regulation is 3 staff for 10 babies under 18 months old, 1 for every 2 toddlers (18-30 months) and 1 for every 8 children aged 30 months-5 years)
4. Did the children appear happy, content and engaged in play and learning?
5. Were there adequate toys, books, activities for each age level?

6. Was I given a calendar of what of special days, activities, events and other important info?

7. Were fire safety precautions well executed with EXIT signs and fire extinguishers?

8. Were things like lunch/snack menus and weekly calendar publicly displayed?

9. Do staff appear experienced?

10. Is my tour guide welcoming my questions with open arms and giving me the answers I want?

11. Can I picture my child coming at this daycare

Age	*Adult:Child Ratio*	*Maximum # children*
Infant (under 18 months old)	3 to 10	10
Toddlers (18 mos-before 30 mos)	1 to 5	15
Preschool (30 mos – before 6 yrs)	1 to 8	16
Kindergarten	1 to 13	26
Grade school	1 to 15	30

Questions to ask daycare centre director

1)How does a a child learn? (I will reveal the correct answer when I get to the part on hiring a nanny...and yes, I will pose this question for home childcare provider as well)

2) How old is the centre?

3) What are your overturn of staff? (If the staff overturn is fairly frequent, I would think twice sending my child there)

4) What are the staff's experience with children? (qualifications yes, but when it boils down to it, I believe experience is the most important component)

5) What is a typical day for the children?

6) What kind of communication do you have with parents (i.e. Newsletter, communication book)

7) How do you deal with food allergies?

8) What is the range of activities the children participate in?

9) How do you discipline?

10) Do you allow kids if they are not potty trained, or if they have a runny nose or cough? (Personally, I would definitely say Yes to the first question, and it would depend if the cold was severe or not to keep them home when the sniffles come around)

11) What is the plan responding to illness?

12) Are children with special needs fully integrated? If there is no discussion about an ECE Resource Teacher...move on to the next daycare centre interview.

13) How much outdoor play do they have?

14) Will I be charged if my child is sick due to illness or we are away on vacation?

15) What is the evacuation plan?

16) Do you have any questions for me?

Q&A with recent 2016 RECE Graduate: Mariah

Q: Why did you want to be an RECE?

Mariah: After high school I actually went to school at Wilfrid Laurier University studying Political Science and Global Studies. After 2 years I realized neither of these paths was going to take me to where I wanted to be. I wanted to be able to have a family and return to a job that wouldn't have hired someone younger and better than me while I was gone. When I thought about my life I realized working with children had always been a passion of mine, the ECE program seemed like my best option at the time to guide me in that direction.

Q: How many placements did you have?

Mariah: I had four placements throughout my time in the program

Q: Where were they?

Mariah: My first placement was in a Preschool class, my second was in a toddler class, my third was in a kindergarten class, and my fourth and best was at the Early Year Centre.

Q: What were the similarities/differences between them?

Mariah: I found that when I was in the daycare setting I had the ability to build stronger relationships with the children. You spend the majority of the day down on the floor playing, learning new things and guiding them. When you are in the classroom setting it is much like when you or I went to school they sit at tables, do lessons as a group, and have scheduled activities. Less time for you to get to spend that one on one time. When I was at the Early Years Centre of course this was a very different program; the parents were very involved and had to participate, what I found though was that my cooperating teacher there wanted me to succeed, she wanted to teach me what others had failed to teach her. She encouraged me to go further and to reach my potential.

Q: What are your evaluations from these placements?

Mariah: Each Centre was given the same evaluation. Each Centre gave very different evaluations. My first Centre gave me an overwhelmingly positive evaluation. I had felt I did great, but struggled to recover all level 4's (highest mark) as it gives you nothing to strive for, but also makes you wonder if they even paid attention to you.

My second Centre was frustrating as my evaluation was done by multiple people, my first evaluation was done by one teacher, my second evaluation done by another as my cooperating teacher had swapped partway through. This is frustrating as neither one matched the other. Did I do well? Yes, however I didn't get a clear picture of what to work on.

My third placement was agonizing and I was very disappointed. The communication was terrible. I had my cooperating teacher along with the Kindergarten teacher and they seemed to have a secret language that was not shared with me, so no one communicated with me, however when I tried to communicate they didn't share it either. So I did fine, but was thoroughly disappointed in that.

My final evaluation at the Early Years Centre was amazing. My cooperating teacher and I had an amazing relationship. We were open and honest the whole placement. She gave me chances to be independent. We talked each day about goals, what we hoped for, and where we planned on ending things. She gave me honest and great feedback, and made me realize my true potential. After my second 2 placements I had honestly begun to hate the program, however my cooperating teacher at the Early Years Centre gave me my love for children back, and gave me hope that I had made the right decision.

Q: What would you recommend a parent look for in a daycare facility?

Mariah: Make sure you talk to the teacher in your child's room. It is so important for you to have an open relationship with the teacher. The only way we are able to support you to our greatest ability is if you allow us to. Each child who walks into our room is loved and cared for to the highest standard, but only if you let a relationship ship grow. Be open about what happens at the program. We are never going to put your child at risk but it is so important to give them the chances to take risks. Always approach the staff if you she questions, don't jump to conclusions before you hear the whole story. But honestly be open and build a relationship with your child's teacher.

Q: **What does every RECE need to have for employment: ECE certification, First Aid/CPR and a Police Check?**

Mariah: Correct, along with a health and safety program for your particular Centre.

Q&A with current RECE: Holly

Q: Why did you want to be an RECE?

Holly: I love children, but it wasn't my first choice. THE PAY IS SO POOR!!!!!!!! And, it's a tough job.

Q: How long have you been an RECE?

Holly: I have been an RECE for 15 years.

Q: How many daycare centres have you worked at?

Holly: I've worked at two centres: Peekaboo Childcare and Kids and Company, Waterloo. I am no teaching full day Kindergarten with the Waterloo Region District School Board.

Q: How many children can a daycare centre hold?

Holly: Depends on the size/square footage of the centre.

Q: How many staff at a typical daycare centre?

Holly: Depends on the size of the centre.

Q: What would you recommend a parent look for in a daycare facility?

Holly: A parent should know what they are looking for and whats important to them (French, sign language, arts, science, clean centre, turn over on staff, etc.)

Q: What does every RECE need to have for employment: ECE certification, First Aid/CPR and a Police Check?

Holly: Valid registration with the College of ECE (costs $150 per year. Admin and registration fees are more at start up.

Q: About OneList....does it actually work? I have heard so much negativity from it, It hasn't worked for many people.

Holly: I have only used OneList for my son in the Extended-day program at his school. The only thing I can say is that it's not very user friendly from an ECE in Extended Day, and as a parent using it.

Ok, you have interviews with daycare centres lined up, you have your checklist, you have your questions. You're set to go!

I know you will make the very best decision of which daycare centre that will fit the needs for your family.

CHAPTER 4

Home Day Care

On my 20 minute walk from home to work each day, I can count 9 home daycare providers....a combination of licensed and private home daycares... that's more than coffee shops! Home childcare providers, no matter if they are licensed or unlicensed are a hot commodity, especially if they are highly recommended and hard to get in. I heard of a lady who had her son in home daycare, but when she went on maternity leave, she kept paying the provider to keep her spot for when she needed her.

Heather of Kitchener, Ontario is one of the most popular private home daycare providers I have come in contact with in Kitchener. Heather follows the regulations set out by the Ontario Government based on Bill 10 the Childcare Modernization Act. I recently asked her if she had availability for a few families who were needing care and was asking me for recommendations. Heather said unfortunately she didn't, she said *"Three of my families are either just coming off mat leave, going on mat leave, or just gone on mat leave. 2017 is going to be a busy!"*

Denise lives in Guelph, Ontario and has run a private home daycare in her home since 2007. She follows the regulations set out by the Ontario Government based on Bill 10 the Childcare Modernization Act. She has become a very popular provider that families hope to acquire. She absolutely loves her job. Denise takes her job very seriously, and plans the schedule for the week, along with snacks and meals. When she takes the children on a "field trip", she has the parents fill out permission forms. Denise sees herself a home daycare provider for the foreseeable future. Families in Guelph are so lucky!

*Kim of Waterloo, Ontario runs a private home daycare. She follows the regulations set out by the Ontario Government based on Bill 10 the Childcare Modernization Act. says *"I don't "advertise" at all. I don't' take many kids in and I am very particular. I've been fortunate to personally know almost all of my families, or they have been very good friends of someone I know. They received high referrals to join my posse."*

By now you've noticed that I included "follows the regulations set out by the Ontario Government based on Bill 10 the Childcare Modernization Act for each private home daycare provider. This is because it is required by law that they need to state this to parents to let them know know they adhere to the regulations set out by the province of Ontario. Also, private daycare providers are required to put in their window a notice saying "This childcare program is not licensed by the Government of Ontario."

Licensed daycare providers receive a decal sticker from the agency they work for (i.e. Region, Wee Watch) that indicates that their childcare program is licensed by the Government of Ontario.

Glowing, word-of-mouth referrals are the very best recommendations that families can get when searching for a home daycare provider. But if you are new to town, and don't know anyone yet, never fear, there are other ways to find that reputable childcare that you can trust.

For the past 3-4 years, Denise has relied on recommendations that her families give to their friends and neighbours and also from websites like www.daycarebear.com and www.godaycare.com. Denise likes these two websites because they are free to join, and you can add as much detail as you want (hours, rates etc.) Since 2006, Daycarebear.ca has helped more than 18,560 daycare providers fill their available spots. I couldn't find how old godaycare.com was. Both are Canadian-wide.

Another place I know families advertise childcare with is Kijiji. Please be very cautious when you do so. I once advertised with Kijii, but found a majority of people wanted to pay what you would pay a home childcare provider. Denise says that she also advertised with Kijiji, only the first year she was in business. *"I hate when people email from Kijiji asking how much I charge, and not ask what I do with the kids."* I am not surprised with this comment at all. Read some of the ads, I have accumulated the last few months:

> *Urgent: Childcare Needed for 2 children. I am looking for a caring childcare provider to help us with 2 children. Looking forward to hearing from you.*
>
> *Friendly Caregiver needed for Our Infant. We are looking for a childcare provider to help us with our infant. Experience and references are a plus. Looking forward to hearing from you.*
>
> *Seeking daycare. Looking for a person who can provide daycare for me four to five days a week. Please, if you are interested or know someone who may be able to help out, it would be greatly appreciated. Thank you in advance.*
>
> *Hello there. I am a sole parent that is looking for an occasional babysitter for whenever I need time to myself. Hopefully this person will be a sitter that could keep this flexible position. Don't hesitate to ask questions.*

When you advertise for childcare, be clear as to what you are looking for, and word it in a way that potential childcare providers. I'm not saying, don't use Kijiji to find a home childcare provider, I'm just asking you to be very cautious when you do so. I compare Kijiji with OneList....it can work, and it has for some...but not for all.

ADVERTISING FOR CHILDCARE? BE DETAILED.

When you write up an advertisement to acquire childcare, make sure you put as much detail as you can. Basically answer the five W's (well, four W's and one H)

What? What are you seeking? Mention the hours you require.

Who? How many children do you have? What are their ages?

Where? What location do you want childcare to be? State the areas you prefer.

Why? Indicate when you are going back to work, and when you would need care.

How? How can the provider of service help you....that is, how many hours you need.

SAMPLE ADVERTISEMENT

In September 2017 I will be returning to work, and am starting the process of seeking out a home childcare provider that would be able to care for both my son who will be 3 years old, and my daughter who will 14 months. I am a teacher, and would require the hours of 8:00-4:00 Monday-Friday, with Christmas break, March break, and summers off. I would prefer the Auditorium area or Forest Heights area as locations for care. I would like care with the emphasis on learning through play, creativity, and being exposed to fun and educational experiences. I look forward to hearing from you, and chat about the best job in the world: caring for children.

> *There's a nurturing element to all human beings,whenever they themselves have been nurtured, and it's going to be expressed one way or another.*
>
> *~Fred Rogers*

HOME CHILDCARE PROVIDER COURSE

Did you know there is actually a "Home Childcare Provider" course? Conestoga College in Kitchener, Ontario was offering it in the late 1990's. I registered for it, and purchased the textbook "Home Child Care . A Caregivers's Guide". The course was cancelled before it began; not enough enrolment. Realistically, I wasn't surprised. Conestoga doesn't offer such a program any longer.

The textbook, no longer in print, was written by Lee Dunster, the founder of The Child Care Providers Association in Ottawa. It details everything you would need to know about starting a home daycare business: ie: organizing your home, the business side of things like how much you would charge, finding clients (this was way before childcare websites and social media outlets) record keeping. There is however a lot of outdated information included like the childcare regulations for each province. But still, it is still a good resource, nonetheless. You can still find copies around. Try your local library, used book stores, Amazon, or social media outlets to request that book title.

One college that does offer such a program is Mothercraft College in Toronto, Ontario www.mothercraft.ca

Their program has been in existence since 2000. Approximately 1,000 students have gone through the program; 27-30 students per course. This is an in-class program vs online. The fee to take the course is: $325 for the program, and an extra $85 for CPR & First Aid for those who are not currently certified.

Tammy, of Waterloo, Ontario is an RECE, and has both worked in a daycare centre, and now has her own home daycare. I interviewed her about being in the two different positions. Here are her answers:

Q: Why did you want to be an RECE?

Tammy: My mom did home child care in our home when I was 4-18 years old. I loved helping her and just being around children. It's a great way to get to be like a child yourself and I love knowing that I play a huge part in the future of generations to come.

Q: How long have you been an RECE?....Did you always want to be in childcare?

Tammy: I graduated from the ECE program at Conestoga College in 2001. I was hired at a licensed daycare centre about 6 months later. After returning from my maternity leave in 2010 I decided to stay home and run my own daycare so I could stay with my son and spend more time with my two daughters and husband.

I have always wanted to work with children. Growing up I dreamed of becoming a teacher. My first job was babysitting as a teen, then I worked in the child care area at a local women's only gym while taking the ECE program. I never continued on to become a teacher because I started a family and was happy working in child care.

Side note: M: You ARE a teacher when you work with children of any age.

Q: What do you like better, working at home or in daycare centre?

Tammy: Both have their pros and cons. I liked the centre because I was with other adults more often and shared the work load, I had an actual lunch and break time (nap time now is spent cleaning up from the morning and preparing for the afternoon), and I had set hours (home care-if a parent is late there's no one to cover for me).

I prefer home care though. I get to be home when my kids wake up and I walk them to/ from school (along with DC kids), I can make my own hours and take vacations as often as I want (I don't get paid for these days of course, so don't often get much time off), another benefit is that I can take care of things around my home while at work. My DC kids have helped me on occasion to make dinner, clean up the house, plant and weed my garden, wash my car, get groceries...everything is a learning opportunity. It almost sounds like child labour, but the kids love helping out and these are great learning opportunities as well for them.

Q: What was the best and worst thing about working at a day care centre and now as a home daycare provider?

Tammy: Centre- best- I guess the best part was having set hours. It can be a very long day sometimes now as I can start at 7am some days and end at 5/5:30pm. As well my kids have activities in the evening sometimes and if a parent is late it can make us late because unlike a centre there is no one to ask to stay and cover for me if I need to leave.

Worst- the structure. Yes, there is some flexibility but it was more ridged than I feel home based care is. In a day care centre you have set themes and schedules. There are set lunch, outdoor and circle times. With my home care day there is more room for flexibility. I feel I can follow the children's lead better. For example, if they are having a lot of fun playing outside then we might push lunch back a bit or eat outside. Crafts are usually what they are interested in that day and we often go with the flow. I try to stick to the same order of activities for some structure (i.e. Snack, lunch, sleep, play, pick up time) and I give warning of what is coming up next.

Home- Best- being my own boss. I make my own hours, vacation time, schedule for the kids, and my own rates.

Worst- Running a home day care takes up my whole house. Bedrooms are used for napping, basement is used for storage of toys, strollers, extra cots, etc and sometimes play, there are potties and stools in all the bathrooms, baby locks, gates and toys everywhere.

Q: How many daycare centres did you work at before becoming a daycare provider.

Tammy: I worked at 3 different centres but all were for the same company over an 8 year period.

Q: Are you licensed or unlicensed?

Tammy: Unlicensed

Q: What would you recommend a parent look for in a daycare facility?

Tammy: Make sure you first ask for references before you do anything else. Then as you take tours of your ideal centres, ask yourself *"Can I already see that my family's needs would be met."*

Q: What would you recommend a parent look for in a home daycare?

Tammy: You want someone who has the same or similar parenting philosophies as you, someone you feel comfortable with (go for your gut), is trained first aid/CPR, and has excellent references.

Q: Have you been to some daycare centres you would NOT recommend?

Tammy: I did a placement where the kids spent most of the day I front of a TV and the staff were not very engaged with the children (i.e. Stood around just chatting with each other. I had that uncomfortable gut feeling

Q: Did the new rules for Bill 10 Modernization for Childcare change much for you?

Tammy: The bill didn't change a lot for me. My numbers were within the ratio already

FOUND POTENTIAL PROVIDERS?

Alright, you've accumulated a list of potential daycare providers for your child(ren). Now's the time to whittle that list down as you interview each, and see who would be the very best fit for your family.

What to Look For

When you are at potential home daycare provider's homes interviewing them for the most important job in the world, looking after your pride and joy, ask yourself these questions, and make mental notes:

1) Before you go in the house, do you see displayed in the window a notice to indicate this home daycare is follows the Government of Ontario's regulations?

2) Are you warmly greeted when you arrive? With a smile?

3) Is the house clean?

4) What does the playroom look like?

5) Are there adequate toys and games for various age groups of children?

6) Is there artwork displayed?

7) Does the provider sound like she loves her job?

8) Is the provider answering all your questions, without hesitating her answers?

9) Are there smoke detectors, carbon monoxide detectors and fire extinguisher present?

10) Is there a calendar of home daycare activities displayed on the fridge/ am I given a copy as an example?

11) Is there a weekly meal plan displayed on the fridge of snacks and lunch for each day?

12) Are there adequate safety measures (example: child locks, baby gates)?

13) Is the backyard fenced – with adequate age appropriate toys?

My Super Hero (Erick Traplin)

Here he comes runnin' down the hallway, cape flappin' in the breeze
A fierce look upon his face, he's searchin' for mister freeze
He's gonna save the world, from the bad guys
Make it safe for you and me.
Up and down the hall, and in every room
He's making this world, a better place to be.
Here he comes running down the hallway He's a super hero to me
He has goodness in his heart He's brave and oh, so kind
He's got to save the world, and do it all, before bed time.
Here he comes running down the hallway He's a super hero to me
There's no escaping, from his super powers, all the bad guys flee in fear
He's huffin' and he's puffin' as he fights them on
the couch, on the ceiling, on the floor
On the chair and out the door, down the hall into his bath
Till there's not one, bad guy left in here
Here he comes running down the hallway, he's a super hero to me
He has goodness in his heart He's brave and oh, so kind,
He's got to save the world, and do it all, before bed time
Here he comes running down the hallway, he's a super hero to me
He's a super hero to me, he's my super hero,
he's my super hero He's a super hero to me,
He's a super hero to me, He's... a ...super... hero... to... me

Below you will find a list of questions to ask your potential home daycare provider:

QUESTIONS FOR HOME CHILDCARE PROVIDER

1. What is the best way a child learns? (Check out the Nanny section to see answer)
2. How long have you been a home childcare provider?
3. Do you see yourself being a childcare provider for a long time?
4. Why are you a childcare provider?
5. What is your background experience?
6. What hours are you open?
7. How many children do you care for?
8. Is there a late fee if we are late for any reason?
9. Do you charge if my child(ren) do not come because of sickness or holidays?
10. Do you charge if you are sick or take holiday time?
11. How many sick days in a year have you had?
12. Do you have First Aid/CPR? How current is it?
13. Do you have a police check? Are you willing to obtain one?
14. What does your family unit look like?
15. Do you, or other people in the house smoke?
16. What is your daily schedule like?
17. What activities will my child(ren) be participating in?
18. What kind of excursions do you take the children on?
19. What educational goals do you have for young children?
20. Do you provide meals or snacks, or will we be bringing all of our child(ren's) nutritional requirements?

21. What kind of food do you prepare? (Do they say fresh food, or processed food?)

22. How do you manage common child-care discipline? Examples. (i.e. If the child didn't want to put their coat on when it's cold out, or if they refused to eat their lunch.

23. How would you handle daily aggressive behaviour to my child from another child?

24. Describe any difficult situations and how did you handle them?

25. What kind of outdoor time would my child(ren) have?

26. How do you handle children who cry endlessly?

27. How would handle a child who refused to eat?

28. What modes of transportation do you use with the children in your care on a daily basis for outings (i.e. Stroller, car, bus)

29. Do you, or anyone in your household smoke?

30. What children's programs/events do you know about?

31. What is your community involvement?

32. What are your hobbies/interests?

33. Do you have Facebook, Twitter, Instagram...what kinds of content do you post?

34. Will you keep a log/journal of my child's day?

35. What are your favourite children's books?

36. What is your policy on TV watching?

37. May we contact your references?

38. Do you have any questions for us?

Remember Cameron and Jenny? They had a great interview with a home daycare provider. I was sent this about how it went:

"It was good! I think we are quite happy with her. She seems to take it seriously and has theory to back up her practice. The questions were very helpful! She was very happy to see they had questions for her; she indicated not many parents have a list of questions ready"

QUESTIONS FOR REFERENCES

What about the reference? What questions should I ask? Here you go!...

1. How long did have you/did you have _______ as your children's home daycare provider? Did you know _______before she was your child's home daycare provider?

2. How were you recommended to ________?

3. Have you always been felt welcome in ______'s home?

4. When and why did you leave? (if reference is past client)

5. Did/Do you always have a good rapoire with _______?

6. Is _______ easy to get along with/talk to?

7. Does _______ respect your values and culture?

8. How is _______'s home kept on a daily basis?

9. Were/are your child's basic needs met?

10. Does your child get 1:1 attention? How do they relate to ________?

11. Was there any time when your child didn't want to go to daycare?

12. Did/Does your child enjoy coming to daycare?

13. Has your child ever had any complaints?

14. Did/has your child ever been disciplined by _______?

15. Did/does ______ communicate to you on a daily basis through a communication book?

16. Does _______ promptly answer your phone calls, texts or emails throughout the working day?

17. Was/has your child ever had some sort of emergency in ________'s care? How did she deal with it?

18. What kinds of experiences has your child been exposed to?

19. What is your child's favourite/least favourite thing about daycare? What your favourite/least favourite thing?

20. How would you describe ________'s care of children?

21. Is ________ accommodating and flexible for your child's individual needs?

22. How much notice has __________ given you when she was going on vacation, or taking a day off?

23. Has ________ always been dependable and reliable?

24. Were/have you always been happy with the meals and snacks ________ provides?

25. Would you use _______ again for daycare?

Yes every answer has a question

not every question has an answer

that sounds strange, but the anwers still the same

when you search for the whats, and the whys and the wheres

you'll be sure to find something there

So ask your question, don't be shy

Lyrics of "Questions"

~Erick Traplin

The Childcare Provider

Although I'm not their Mother
I care for them each day
I cuddle, sing and read to them
and watch them as they play.
I see each new accomplishment
and help them grow and learn.
I understand their language,
and listen with concern.
They come to me for comfort,
and I kiss away their tears.
They proudly show their work to me,
I give he loudest cheers.
I am not their Mother
but my role is just as strong
I nurture them, and keep them safe,
through maybe not for long.
I know someday the time may come
when we have to part
But I know each child I cared for
is forever in my heart.
-Author Unknown

*I am bawling right now....trying to find the kleenex.

CONTRACT

Your daycare provider should already have a contract she uses for her clients, if she doesn't, I'm not sure if I'd go with her. A daycare provider who is ready with a contract drawn up means she is professional, serious, and cares about her job. A contract is crucial for many reasons. First, it saves both you and your childcare provider a lot of misunderstandings. It is a professional employment document detailing of what to expect. This includes:

-the hours and days of the week for child care is to be provided

-the fee per week (including statutory holidays), and when payment is due (ie weekly, bi-weekly)

-list of conditions of payment in the event of illness or vacation time – for both parties

-personal information about each child being cared for in the family (ie DOB, medical information)

-list of expectations when both parties should notify the other about illness (or that of someone in the provider's household), holiday plans, emergency contact information changes (ie new cell number or email address....wouldn't you hate to forget to give them that, and emergency arises

-a list of what is expected to be the activities in the daily schedule for the childcare provider to deliver

If a child requires daily medication, a separate medications authorization form must be completed. See the resources section of where to find forms you can download and print.

Ok! You have interviews with potential home daycare providers lined up, you have your checklist of what to look for in the home, you have your questions, for both her and her references.

I know you will make the very best decision of which daycare centre that will fit the needs for your family! :)

CHAPTER 5

Nanny

Ah, at last! One of my favourite child related topics there is! I'm biased, what can I say! :)

To date, I have been interviewed 16 times to be a nanny, and that doesn't count all the emails I've received asking for more information, and then never hear from them again.

So, you've read through the chapter on daycare centres, and even though you like all the perks like a play based, but structured program, socialization with other children, unique educational experiences ECE educated staff, outdoors time, nutritious meals and snacks. But, the pitfalls include OneList not working in your favour, and the daycare centres you would want because of the location of your home or workplaces never call when you ready to go back to work, the hours don't fit with your schedule, like once again, Jill Drader's example in the ParentsCanada article.

You've looked into and contemplated on sending your child(ren) to a home daycare, either licensed or unlicensed, but because of the new law of only 2 under 2, and you have either twins, or a 1 yr old and a 2 yr old, and the provider already has a child under 2, so you're S.O.L.

I can't help, but to again state all the Pro's for hiring a Nanny...

Pros

*child doesn't have to get up super early to get to the childcare arrangement. *When I come, Lauren is still in her jammies, having breakfast.

*1:1 attention

*long-term

*flexible

*if a child is sick, a nanny still comes to care for the child (unlike daycare centres or home daycare's)

*less expensive if you have more than one child in care

*tax write-off

I mentioned in the first chapter of how the concept of hiring a nanny is most often misunderstood. I get mixed reactions when I say I am a Nanny:

Oh wow! That's amazing!

Oh man...how could anyone afford a Nanny?

They are so lucky to have you

How did they find you?

Wow....8:30-6:00 pm that's a long day. *I especially find this comment funny....because you, as a parent are saying *'Pffft! Less than 10 hours in a day....try 24/7'.*

Lady in mall: *How many kids do you look after?*

Me: *One*

Lady in mall: *only one...you need to care for more kids than that....how old is the one you have?*

Me: 2 1/2 years old.

Lady in mall: *Oh...well that's enough then. They must drive you crazy, running all over the place.*

Me: *No, she's a great kid. I am very fortunate. I love my job as a Nanny.*

Conversation stopped. And I just rolled my eyes as I walked the other way.

PLACES TO FIND A NANNY

*Word-of-mouth: the best recommendation you can get

*www.canadiannanny.ca

*www.nannyservices.ca

Canadiannanny.ca is what I used to acquire two of the seven families I have worked for. I honestly don't remember how I first stumbled upon this website; but I am ever glad I did! Founded in 2002 by Michelle Scully of Toronto while she was on maternity leave. Canadiannanny has helped to bring world-class top-notch Nannies to literally thousands of families throughout Canada.

Canadiannanny helps you every step of the way to find your perfect match. Both families seeking, and nannies seeking can post a detailed profile of themselves, and what they are looking for, offering. Remember: knowledge is power. Make it as detailed, and as professional as possible. After all, you're serious about finding top notch childcare for your pride and joy. Once potential matches are found: the Nanny or family can contact the other. Look often, as new postings are being added daily. There are also informative blog posts on everything under the sun, child related. Sample questions for the nanny, and for their references are included on the website (not as comprehensive as in this book:), and a brand new feature, not offered when I was active, was for a fee, they can take care of paying your Nanny by direct deposit, Canada Revenue Agency (CRA) registration, calculations of net and gross pay, taxes, CPP, and EI amounts, produce receipts at each pay period, and complete a Record of Employment (ROE).

Nannyservices.ca was launched in 2008, and is basically the very same concept as canadiannanny.ca, just another site you can use to find your Nanny.

I know people who have used both sites to find a Nanny, and all have been very happy with the results.

There are also several agencies that you can acquire a Nanny from, like how Sandra Bratty has always found her nannies from because of the screening process. She raved about Nanniesoncall.ca. ***see the back of the book for a list of other agencies.**

Now if you want to do all the bookkeeping yourself, go ahead....both families that I have worked for thus far who have taken off all these items, and I've been told it's easy peasy...read on, and I will share the business information.

Or, does it sound too complicated or intense? Just remember this: you yourself wants to be paid an hourly wage/salary, with tax, CPP, EI taken off. Treat your Nanny the same way. When you are ready to receive CPP, don't forget that your Nanny you had for your children will also reach the age of retirement, and don't you think she'll appreciate that CPP amounts were taken off her paycheques?

BUSINESS INFO FOR PAYROLL

Here is the info for setting up a business number and payroll account. This needs to be done since you are an employer, and if deductions are not taken off at the source for your Nanny, your employee, you can get into lots of hot water with CRA – not something you want to happen.

The forms to sign (TD1) for payroll deductions can all be accessed from the CRA website.

You will need to visit *www.cra.gc.ca* to set up a payroll account and get a business number. Once you are a registered user - click on links for business, click on "payroll" , click on "payroll deduction online calculator" (PDOC) – bookmark it- it makes it super easy to figure out deductions once you have gross wages calculated. Print off employee summary as well as employer summary.

Hiring a nanny in accordance with the law has many advantages for both you and the employee. One major advantage is you can deduct childcare expenses from your income. The amount you can deduct annually is $7,000 for each child age six and under and $4,000 for each child between seven and 16. If the child is eligible for the disability tax credit, you can deduct $10,000 regardless of the child's age.

One thing I need to mention before you consider hiring a nanny as your childcare arrangement:

YOU WANT IN-HOME CHILDCARE?...... WORK ELSEWHERE

If you are thinking a nanny would be the ideal childcare arrangement for your family, please do not do so if you have a home office and work at home. Personally, I will never work for a family who worked from home day in, day out. I've seen firsthand what a bad idea it can be, even if it's one day because the parent is home sick. Children know their parent (s) are home, and may cause a scene because they want to see Mom/Dad and they are told they are not allowed to. It has proven to be a terrible scene, as the children wanted to go see Mom, and they couldn't. It ends up to be more of a headache than a peaceful, uninterrupted nap. If you do have a nanny, and you take off a day because of illness, if at all possible, try and sleep at your parent's houses, a friend's, a neighbour....just to be out of the house. Think of it this way: you wouldn't want to have the feeling of having your boss steps away from you all day, everyday; it would make you uneasy, self-conscious, and thinking that your every move is being watched. Don't do that to your nanny, I guarantee you she will not enjoy her job as much if she has you in the house day in. Recently, I saw Jazmin, (you will read more about her shortly) and she was with a new family. I knew the youngest child she had been looking after wouldn't be of school age yet, so I inquired about that family. She said both the parents now worked from home, so her services weren't needed anymore, because now they are home. Good for those employers, they made the right decision. If you want to employ a nanny, work outside of the home.

In April 2011, I initially had my profile up on canadiannanny.ca for 3 months, I had approximately 8 people who replied asking for more information, or I saw their profile and told them what I do as a Nanny. NOTHING was happening. One day I was so frustrated, and said *"Screw this!"* and deleted my profile (I mean, put it to inactive:) Then, a few weeks later, I thought, *"What the heck, I'll put it up again"* and four hours later, Sarah emails me saying she loved my profile and wanted to meet with me.

In July 2014, I went back on canadiannanny once again to find my next job. A few people found my profile, and wanted to meet with me, and three interviews happened in the span of a week and a half. I had one family who was interested in me, but for some reason, I couldn't put my finger on it, I couldn't see myself working there, it just didn't feel right. Remember reading in the Hiring Childcare chapter about not pulling any punches? The family with the twins did that to me. And the third, well, they didn't seem to know what they wanted.

I feel so fortunate that these families didn't work out. Because I received this message on canadiannanny.ca:

> *Hi Melissa!*
>
> *I am starting the process of looking for a nanny for my daughter when I return to work in the fall. She is not quite a year old. Your profile appeals to me, as I currently attend programming at both the library and the market, and I would like that programming to continue.*
>
> *Would you be interested in further discussion? The hours would be 8:30/9- 6 pm, 3 days a week until March, then an increase to 4 days. Tentative days are Wednesday, Thursday and Friday at the minimum. I am looking for a long term placement as well.*
>
> *Look forward to hearing from you!*
>
> *Catherine*

After a few more email attempts to get me to agree to a meet n' greet (remember, I was waiting for other families to get back to me with a yes or no answer), as soon as Catherine held the door open for me to come in for our interview, I just knew I'd be working here. *I got a little choked up as I typed this. Lauren and I have a bond like no other.

NANNY-SHARING

Nanny-sharing is when one nanny works for two or more families at the same time, caring for all or some of the children from each family (depending on if they are in school or not) at once. This nanny is given a higher salary, but it proves to be cheaper for the families as they pay less when the salary or wage per hour is split into however many families are involved. My last position was a Nanny-share arrangement. I cared for a 3 yr old throughout the day, and I did before/after school and PA Day care for his 7 yr old sister, and a 4 yr old from another family.

LIVE-IN CAREGIVER PROGRAM

Since writing the "How to Land Your Mary Poppins" article in 2012, the Live-in Caregiver Program changed as of November 30, 2014. To see the changes, and if you are eligible to hire a live-in caregiver from overseas http://www.cic.gc.ca/english/work/apply-who-caregiver.asp

A majority of Nannies who work through the Live-in Caregiver Program in Canada come from the Philippines or the Caribbean. Au Pair is another word term for Live-in Nanny.

I have met some pretty fantastic nannies from overseas working for families right here in Kitchener, Ontario.

Jazmin, from the Philippines is one of them, and she is the best of the best. I love watching her interact with the children under her care. I interviewed Jazmin on her role as a Nanny from an international country. Here is our Q&A.

Q: When and why did you become a Nanny in Canada vs another country?

Jazmin: After working for 3 years in Hong Kong as a Nanny, I applied and was hired directly as a live-in caregiver for Canada in June 2008. Canadians are polite, diverse, kind hearted people. Canada has a good live-in caregiver program. After completion of 24 months of working as a live-in caregiver, we are allowed to to apply for an open work permit, and permanent residency will follow. We can even sponsor our own family to come live with us in Canada. I don't have any other country in mind to apply to be a Nanny other than Canada, after my time in Hong Kong.

Q: How many families have you worked for in Canada?

Jazmin: I have worked for four families. The first two families I had in Canada had extended contracts, meaning more than a year. The third family ended up moving to Mississauga, because of their employment position. I was offered a higher salary to follow them to Mississauga to be their live-out Nanny, but I wouldn't be able to handle the drive from Waterloo to Mississauga and back each day. I did however assist them to find a Nanny in Mississauga for them. My fourth family is the one I have currently, since June, 2016.

Q: Can you tell me how the Live-in Caregiver Program works for you? What does it all entail?

Jazmin: Canada has the best program for live-in caregivers. Canada is ranked 3rd by Filipinos country to work in. I know 10 years ago, there was a flood of Filipino Nannies working in Saudi Arabia, and Hong Kong. Even now, there are many, many, Filipino Nannies want to work in Canada, and have permanent residence here. I helped three of my friends to be hired directly as a live-in caregiver, and now they have their papers.

Q: What are your living/working arrangements?

Jazmin: Since I am a permanent resident, I now live on my own, not in the family's home. I am a live-out Nanny now, and because of that, I receive a higher salary from my many years when I was a live-in caregiver. In addition, we have the choice to enter into a contract for however long we can stay with a family, and give two weeks notice if we decide to leave, or if the family no longer needs our services; whichever comes first. For me, it makes no difference how long a family needs me, as I am a widow, and I do have my own kids, so the more hours the better, as long as I can manage it.

Q: How many hours a day do you work? How much time do you get off?

Jazmin: It depends on how long the employer needs you. For me, I ask for no less than 40 hours a week; but at the present time I am working 42 hours a week, and am paid bi-weekly. My days off are on the weekends, but if they need me at that time, I require them to tell me ahead of time, and we just offset or swap the days.

Q: What are your duties as a Nanny?

Jazmin: My household chores are light housekeeping, but my main concentration are the children. My employers have full trust in me and allow me to initiate what our our daily activities and excursions, making sure they are learning while they are having fun. I also set up play dates. I give them updates what our activities are by sending pictures and videos to them while they are at work. They really appreciate my initiative.

Q: Do you see yourself being a Nanny in Canada for years to come?

Jazmin: I did try to work outside the Nanny world for almost 7 months, but I found it more tiring and less money to gain. Of course, if given the chance, I want to upgrade my studies, but for now I have my own kids with me to support. Once my kids have stable jobs, that will be time for me to study again. I am a University graduate with a Bachelor of Sciences in mass communications, with a major in Broadcasting in the Philippines. I did work as a radio broadcaster for 10 years in the Philippines (both as a news reporter and an anchor on the news), but I had no choice but to work abroad to support my children since my husband died when he was 27 years of age of liver cancer.

Q: Did you have a hard time adjusting when you came to Canada?

Jazmin: I didn't find it hard whatsoever working in Canada. Canadian people are very good. I am flexible, understanding, and most of all unending patience, working with people of all walks of life. If you first worked in a country like Hong Kong, it was the best training ground before coming to any other country. A majority of employers in Hong Kong treat their

Nannies as slaves; you're on call 24 hours a day, but only get paid for 8 of those hours, and you only get one day off a week.

Q: Have you always had a great relationship with your families you've cared for?

Jazmin: Yes! Communication is still alive with all former employers! I am pleased to say that all of my employers have given me excellent referrals to prospective employers. I still help with babysitting on the weekends or helping to maintain their home. It is not about the money we receive, but it is the care and the love we share to the family, especially to the children. It warms your heart when see that, and appreciate your effort. My employers have said this both in words and gifts that have been given to me. I treat my employer's children as my own. I am super hands on.

**I can attest, Jazmin is super hands on, and treats the children she cares for as her own. Jazmin is a fantastic Nanny, Canada; Waterloo Region specifically is so lucky to have her caring for our future generation of adults. We're in excellent hands!

Think back to when I was talking about how a nanny is a serious profession. In 2010, when I started looking for my next position, I sent the following to potential families; and in which I've been told was extremely appreciated, and ultimately that's what got me the jobs. Remember, the "being detailed" part.

> *Dear ______________________*
>
> *Thank you so much for considering me as a possible nanny for your children. I am excited to be looking for a new position and meeting a new family. I have previously nannied for a total of three families...and all together 6 children....and a total of over 12 years as a Nanny. The first family had two children, and I cared for the youngest...Lauren from when she was 16 months until she had just turned 6 years of age. Our activities included early learning at home with a variety of activities, baking, playdates, library programs, community centre programs. She did not go to Junior Kindergarten because she had me...in Kindergarten I volunteered in her classroom on a weekly basis. The second family, I cared for a 16 month old girl named Charliese. We attended playgroups, library programs, parks, etc. I cared for their second*

daughter Alyssa, from when the time she was 9 months until she was 13 months of age, when Mom was on maternity leave with their third child. My third, and most recent family, I cared for their first daughter Emma, from when she was 10 months until June 2009, when she was close to 4 1/2 years of age. Her sister Lauren, came into my care in April 2009 for three months from the ages of 12 months-14 months. The various activities with this family were Kids Hop! at Kitchener Market (I am a 4 year attendee to this awesome children entertainment hour!), library, playgroup, baking, make playdough, playdates, Adult &Tot and Adult&Tot Advanced Swimming lessons, and I was very involved in Emma's parent participating preschool (Moppet Preschool), where I learned a wealth of knowledge.

I have lived most of my life in the East end of Kitchener. I live with my parents and youngest sister. I have one dog, a Goldendoodle named Daisy. I love films and I am an avid reader; books are a passion as is my writing. I enjoy writing and am working on writing a book, as well as have had the good fortune of publishing several magazine articles of topics pertaining to children.

I attended Conestoga College in Kitchener for both Educational Assistant 1, and Writing Children's Literature. I have also become a Kindersigns Instructor, teaching sign language to my charges, and I continue attending workshops and seminars of child related topics to keep up to date, and learn new skills/techniques. I am certified in Emergency First Aid and CPR and I have a current police records check.

I have always worked with children and cared for them. I began babysitting when I was twelve for neighbourhood children. In high school I performed my co-op at Rosemount Public School in a classroom of students with severe disabilities. My experience with children with disabilities is extensive from volunteering with Extend-a-Family, now an employee as a Special Services at Home Worker, financially supporting KidsAbility Centre for Child Development (I am actually a former client from late 1970's) and supporting the Waterloo Region Down syndrome Society at special events. My other volunteer has been with several primary classrooms, Children's Liturgy/Sunday School Coordinator and Teacher, World Youth Day 2002 in Waterloo Region, Youth Group Leader. Before I began nannying full time, I was a Child Care Worker at Exclusively Women's Fitness Centre in the Childcare room.

I am looking for a position where I can be a full charge nanny, helping to shape the physical, social and emotional development of the children in my care. I would like a position where I am seen as an important part of the child's life as that is how I view my role. I want the children in my care to grow into wonderful individuals and I want to do all I can to help in that process. My job isn't just to care for the child's safety and provide them with meals and the opportunity for play, but to also help them develop socially and emotionally and to learn respect and life skills. I believe that children need routines, boundaries and fun! I believe in reading lots of books, getting dirty, baking, painting, making sand castles, dancing to the music and splashing in puddles after a rainstorm. I believe in giving children reasonable choices and allowing them to express their own opinions.

I am seeking a position where I will have the ability to do outings with the children including play dates with other children, outings to places such as the Kids Hop! at The Kitchener Market, the library, community centre, playgroup, and city parks. I would also like the opportunity to take children to activities on the bus, as I do not drive, and this has always worked out great, and the children love going on the bus. One of the most important parts of my work is ensuring that the children are given the opportunity to socialize, meet new people, and develop friendships, regardless of their age.

My expected rate of pay would be between $13-$15 an hour.

Being a nanny is not just a job to me; I take it very seriously and want only the best for the children in my care. I value my position, my work and what a large responsibility it is.

I look forward to meeting you. Please contact me at any time with questions or concerns.

Sincerely,

Melissa Martz

Since writing this seven years ago, I am now caring for my 7th family, I still do a majority of these activities and outings, and I now power walk in a multitude of races each year. And, I am close to celebrating my 12th year taking kids to KidsHop! And yes, Daisy is still around:)

In March 2016, Erick Traplin released his 8th Children's Cd entitled "My Magic Carpet". This song instantly became my very favourite. I think of Lauren every time I listen to it.

"FOREVER AND A DAY"

Written By Erick Traplin & Ronald A Roy

Take a cup of tenderness
add a little love
shake it up, throw in a dash of wild and crazy
and you've got a winning recipe for

Twinkling eyes that shine so bright
a crooked little smile
a happy laugh that goes on and on for miles
no wonder I keep on singing

I'm going to love you, love you forever and a day
I'm going to love you, love you forever and a day

Sun shines, shines so bright
with you in my life
and I know whenever I am around you
I will feel just right

You've got my number
you can call anytime
and I will come runnin' as fast as I can
I'm so happy that you are mine, and

I'm going to love you, love you forever and a day
I'm going to love you, love you forever and a day

You pick me up when I feel down
you've taught me more about life just being around
forgive the past, forget the future
I want to spend all my nows with you for sure

You've got my number you can call anytime
and don't you know I'm so happy that you are mine, and
I'm gonna love you forever and a day.

Ok, you have found potential candidates through referrals, www.canadiannanny.ca or www.nannycare.ca viewed their resumes and cover letters. Now comes the all important job of interviewing them to find the best of the best.

QUESTIONS TO ASK A POTENTIAL NANNY

1.What is the best way a child learns? (Right answer: Play)

2.How long have you been a live-in or live-out Nanny? Why are you one?

3. What is your experience?

4. How flexible are you in terms of hours?

5. What kinds of foods would you prepare for toddler and preschoolers?

6. How many sick days in a year have you had?

7. Do you have First Aid/CPR? How current?

8. Do you have a police check? Are you able to obtain one?

9. What has your daily schedule been like with other families?

10. What activities have you participated with children in your care?

11. Describe a difficult situation and how you handled it.

12. How do you manage a child who cries endlessly and are inconsolable?

13. How do you handle a person at the door claiming to be a relative and wants entry?

14. How do you manage common child-care discipline? Examples. (i.e. If the child didn't want to put their coat on when it's cold out, or if they refused to eat their lunch?

15.Have you ever had an emergency situation while children are in your care?

16. What kind of outdoor activities would you do with the children?

17. How do you deal with aggressive behaviour?

18. Do you drive, or would you bus/walk to activities?

19. What children's programs/events do you know about?

20. What is your community involvement?

21. What are your hobbies/interests?

22. Do you have Facebook, Twitter, Instagram...what kinds of content do you post?

23. What educational goals do you teach children? What ways do you use to teach these concepts?

24. How do you handle children who cry endlessly and are inconsolable?

25. Do you take holidays?

26. How many sick days have you had in a year?

27. Will you contribute keeping the house tidy? What tasks will you or won't you do?

28. Do you smoke?

29. What are some of your favourite children's books?

30. May we contact your references?

31. Do you have any questions for us?

REFERENCES

Now, I hope you don't have any candidates that takes a cue from Mary Poppins saying she never gives references, that it's a very old fashioned idea. Well, my dear birthday buddy Julie Andrews, it is not an old fashioned idea. References are an absolute must! This is your chance to ask others who have entrusted your candidate to the care of their children, and find out if what both the nanny's answers to your questions, and yours gut feeling match, and it would indeed be a great fit.

Please note, that if your candidate does not wish to give you the name of their most recent employer (another family) hear her out first, before writing her off, or making assumptions. This very thing happened to me... let me explain: I got the impression that a previous employer did not like the baby or toddler stage, and voiced their opinion and scoffed when I would mention how I love looking after babies and toddlers. So, when I was actively searching for my current position, I did not include this individual as one of my references. I explained my reasoning for not including her, saying that even though I know she would have given me an excellent reference, I just couldn't include her name, knowing her thoughts about caring for babies and toddlers. Each one of my interviewers the summer of 2014, agreed with my decision, all saying "Good call!"

QUESTIONS FOR REFERENCES

What about the references? What questions should I ask? Here you go!...

1. How long did have did you have _______ as your children's home Nanny? Did you know _______before she was your child's Nanny?

2. How were you recommended to ________?

3.Why do you no longer employ ________?

4. Did you always have a good rapport with _______?

5. Is _______ easy to get along with/talk to?

6. Does _______ respect your values and culture?

7. Was your home tidy when you came home at night?

8. Were/are your child's basic needs met?

9. How do they relate to ________?

10.Was there any time when your child didn't want your Nanny to come/take over (if live-in)?

11. Did your child enjoy their time with ____________?

12. Has your child ever had any complaints?

13. Did/has your child ever been disciplined by _______?

14. Did ______ communicate to you on a daily basis through a communication book?

15. Does _______ promptly answer your phone calls, texts or emails throughout the working day?

16. Did your child ever had some sort of emergency in ________'s care? How did she deal with it?

17. What kinds of experiences has your child been exposed to?

18. What is your child's favourite/least favourite thing about _______ as their Nanny? What your favourite/least favourite thing?

19. How would you describe ________'s care of children?

20. Is ________ accommodating and flexible for your child's individual needs?

21.How much notice has ___________ given you when she was going on vacation, or taking a day off?

22. Has ________ always been dependable and reliable?

23. Were you always been happy with the meals and snacks ________ provides?

24. Would you use _______ again as your children's Nanny?

A FEW OTHER DETAILS

*Don't forget to give your nanny a letter stating they are able to seek out medical treatment for their child if need be when they are in the nanny's care.

*Consider packing a first aid kit to keep in the stroller basket for outings. One of my previous employers had one made up in the stroller, and was it ever handy for skinned knees that needed a band-aid kiss.

*Your local newspaper often has photographers out and about around town, and might ask your nanny if they could take a photo of her and your child(ren) at a random location or event, and it being published in the next day's paper. Let your nanny know if that would be Ok or not, and if you only want first names published, or if the last name can be as well. **I actually thought of this, and asked my employers...they were vey impressed and appreciated that I thought of that and asked. It hasn't happened thus far...but you never know!**

*make sure your nanny is introduced to your neighbours. They can be a lifesaver on many occasions. Thinking back to all my positions as a nanny, I knew neighbours at each home I was at. That has served me well: I had to get a house key when I accidentally locked us out of the house (the front door locked automatically), I've borrowed eggs for baking, I've borrowed a plunger to unclog the toilet, I've had to get a diaper. And, if there was ever an emergency, it's comforting to know you could get assistance from neighbours right away.

CONTRACT

Drawing up an employment contract between you and your nanny is the perfect way to show you are serious and care about this position you are entrusting this individual to the care of your children, and is a written document of what you want childcare to be for your children. This contract will house all the details for employment, complete with:

-date to start

-hours

-expected duties

-information on overtime, vacation time and sick days

-pay

-reasons for termination

Each party signs and each keeps a copy for their records.

SAMPLE CONTRACTS

Here's a few places to find a sample contract you can download and print off for your personal use.

http://d3c1grj748hoip.cloudfront.net/assets/canadian-nanny/guide/downloads/CanadianNanny_SampleEmploymentAgreement

a60e155f5d33fb43366dd7b1f8efe905f345274a1e06b893848eab-412f6e574a.pdf

https://www.care.com/homepay/do-you-need-a-nanny-contract-07101004

Or, our friend Pinterest has oodles of sample contracts ideas that you can download and print as well.

OK! You have your potential nanny candidates, you have interview questions and reference questions.

I know you will make the very best decision for your family! Happy Mary Poppins searching!

CHAPTER 6

Firing Your Childcare Provider

What happens when you have to fire your childcare provider? How do you go about it?

I'm fortunate I've never been fired from a childcare position, except for that time in high school, I guess you'd say I was fired. However, I think it felt like I was fired, just the way I was given the cold shoulder the duration of my temporary nanny position between February -April 2011. I was hired to help care for a toddler who had some high medical needs along with her 2 yr old sister, and a newborn baby. One day I could not find any diapers on the main floor whatsoever, so I went upstairs to the bedrooms to find some. I did find in their bedroom where I often would get the medical supplies, but this particular day the door was closed, and I went in anyway. Oh boy, the Mom did not like that at all. She sent me a very nasty email...I responded by apologizing, but that I couldn't find any diapers whatsoever downstairs. I always felt on edge after that, as if she really didn't want me around. She wouldn't even let me clean up when I came one day, and the main floor looked like a tornado went through it. As soon as their SSAH

(Special Services at Home) money ran out, I was never asked to come again.

If you suspect something is going on with the daycare centre, home daycare or in your home with your nanny, send out some feelers and ask questions first, before you jump to conclusions. There are various ways you can do this:

-ask your child if anything is going on. Young children are very honest, they don't lie.

-ask other parents at the daycare centre or home daycare if they have noticed anything

-again with your neighbours...I'm not talking about the nosy parkers, but they can be your best security if you have in-home childcare.

-Nanny Cam

If nothing turns up, and you still have this gut feeling, begin asking questions to the source. Depending on the answer, you might just fire them right then and there. Use your own good judgment. Now, I know I promised not to fill this book with negativity, but here are some examples of scenarios that have played out...and then appreciate the fantastic childcare you have! I hope none of you will ever have to go through what these parents have had to go through. Oh yeah, and I hope you don't get the childcare provider Jill thought she had for her children, and the day she was to start, she phoned to say she couldn't come because her cat was sick.

A few years ago I was asked what my availability was because an acquaintance I knew, knew a family whose nanny they were suspecting was drinking the alcohol from the liquor cabinet. I don't know whatever happened with that family, how that nanny was fired, I know the way they knew for sure was they set out "traps" to catch her by measuring how much liquor was in certain bottles, and then come home after work and measure again to see if there was any gone.

In 2000, I received a phone call one night from my employer, and questioned me pretty confused about several long distance charges that had been racked up. I reassured her that if I ever made a long distance phone call, I would ask first, and she knew that. After my employer told me a few of the dates these calls were made, I reminded her that those days I wasn't even working, because of my grandmother's funeral.

Those long distance charges were pointed to an evening teenage babysitter they had. Remember the days of MSN? Apparently this girl met a guy on there who lived in Nova Scotia. She didn't' want her parents to know she was calling him, so she did so at my employer's home. To give her the benefit of the doubt, she most likely didn't understand how phone bills worked. Weeks later when I was doing some nighttime childcare for them, I too was talking on the phone, and as I hung up, I said *"I was just talking to my friend in Tokyo"*. They both laughed!

Susan had to fire her son's childcare provider. This person came highly recommended from a friend, as well as a few other people who had her as their children's childcare provider. Susan could see why she was highly recommended for the first little while; she was excellent. Then her circumstances changed and became pregnant with her third child. She became fatigued and was falling asleep on the job. Her daughter, who has about 8 years old was jealous of her 2 year old brother, and it also translated to Susan's son. One day when the childcare provider had fallen asleep, the daughter got hold of razor blades and slashed the back of both her brother's and her son's hands, and cut her son's cheek down to his neck, where it could have cut an artery. The childcare provider woke up and just put a bandaid on her son's cheek...going the wrong direction. She, herself had a doctor's appointment, and left a friend to stay with the boys.

When Susan picked her son up, she was horrified at the lack of judgment and irresponsibility and the family dynamic that had developed. Susan fired her on the spot, and asked her husband to pick up their son's belongings the next day. Susan rushed her son to the ER – he required seven stitches, and the medical personnel were shocked at how many hours had gone by with such a significant cut. Her son, now an adult still has a scar.

Normally, cases like this reported at the ER would first have had questioned the parent by FACS (Family and Children's Services) before being allowed to take them home. But somehow, that didn't happen. But Susan reported it herself to FACS. A few weeks later Susan noticed that lady's house was for sale, and had heard she left town. Susan doesn't know know if the authorities found her or not.

The first home daycare provider *Marcie had for her son *Jack fired him because he threw his food on the floor, said he pooped too much, and that she was starting not to like him. She wrote Marcie a letter, and as soon as Marcie read it, Jack was pulled out of that daycare, although she gave Marcie a week before Jack wasn't welcome anymore. Pretty cute, eh!

Feeling rushed finding care ASAP (I know, I know, she didn't have this book to guide her), Marcie went with a lady down the street from her because she was desperate to find someone. Jack was there for six months, then he clotheslined the provider's son, and he was fired on the spot. The provider put all of Jack's belongings out on her lawn, left the house and made her husband give Marcie's husband Jeff a note. Marcie relayed to me *"you don't want to know what I did next!"*

This story had a happy ending in the end...she found an awesome daycare centre, one of which she raves about still to this day. Kudos to you, Owl Childcare Services!

*names changed

*Karen had employed international au pairs for her children ever since her first child (now 6) was a year old. Out of all of the au pairs they've employed, there were two that had to be let go.

She said *"when we let the first gal from France go, we just said it wasn't working out, and gave her an end date, paid her until that time, and I offered to help her get her bookings arrangement to go home if she wished."*

The last au pair they had was a male from Germany. The reasoning for his departure was a very different situation. This guy was found to have been putting hidden cameras throughout their house . Karen says in hindsight she should have phoned the RCMP and charged him with voyeurism. But, she wanted to be kind, give a second chance, and show forgiveness, which is what she did. When the hidden cameras were found, Karen gave him the opportunity to be honest and come clean, but he chose to lie. *"My husband drove him to the bus station to take a Greyhound to the hotel by the airport, since the flight was international, it would not be until the next day, and I didn't want him to be in my home any longer. I had family members pack up his belongings, and his luggage met him at the hotel."*

Karen contacted this guy's family to let them know he was coming.

*name changed

Do I hear a *"Wow"* coming from a majority of you? Yes, Wow! Can I ask that when you do find the childcare arrangement that is second to none, and the very best fit for your family, that you appreciate them, and don't' take them for granted. You don't want to end up with a childcare arrangement that mirrors one of these examples.

LETTING GO

Being "let go" is different than being fired. Yes, I know, you are "let go" when you are fired too, but I think of when I have been "let go" from nanny positions, it wasn't because I was fired, I was because various factors came into play.

-child started school full-time (at that time it was Grade 1, because Kindergarten was still half days... this was from my first nanny job, can you tell?)

-employer went on maternity leave

-employer lost his job

-family moved to a different city

Whatever the reason for the change, one thing remains constant: everyone involved – including you, your child, other children (or adults) at the daycare or programs you went to on a weekly basis will all be affected by the change. I know I've cried at endings to positions where I was ultra close with the children. I know when I have to leave my current nanny position will be extremely hard. I've already told a very good friend of mine that I will be crying on their shoulder when it's the end. With the care and support of your relationship with your childcare provider, your friends and family, you will get through this change, it might just take a little time. I think it's safe to say that it's a little like dealing with a death, you are upset because you won't see that person anymore that you've been close to...it's hard.

RESOURCES

Finding and hiring childcare as you can see is the most important, but also most daunting, time consuming task you will undertake in your child's young life if you should decide to go back to work after maternity leave. I hope that the information you've read, and the resources in this chapter you can tap into to make sure you have made the best decision for your family.

CHILDCARE REGULATIONS PROVINCE TO PROVINCE

I found this quite interesting about the differences and similarities throughout each province. I really thought it would be across the board, didn't you?

http://www.cbc.ca/marketplace/blog/compare-provincial-regulations-and-guidelines#BC

LICENSED CHILDCARE WAIT LISTS PROVINCE TO PROVINCE

British Columbia: http://www2.gov.bc.ca/gov/content/family-social-supports/caring-for-young-children/child-care

Alberta: http://humanservices.alberta.ca/family-community/child-care.html

Saskatchewan: obtain a list of licensed childcare centres/day homes by contacting the Childcare Regional office closest to you.

Manitoba: https://onlinechildcareregistry.gov.mb.ca/occrweb

Ontario: Google OneList for your community

Quebec: For those living in Montreal: www.montrealdaycare.com

http://www.childcarecanada.org/resources-canadian-parents/quebec

Nova Scotia: Directly contact daycare centres of your choosing to put your child on the waiiting list.

New Brunswick: Directly contact daycare centres of your choosing to put your child on the waiiting list.

Newfoundland: Directly contact daycare centres of your choosing to put your child on the waiiting list.

Prince Edward Island: http://www.gov.pe.ca/infopei/index.php3?number=1038160&lang=E

Northwest Territories: http://findingqualitychildcare.ca/northwest-territories

Yukon: http://www.hss.gov.yk.ca/pdf/licensedchildcarecentres.pdf

http://www.hss.gov.yk.ca/pdf/licensedchildcarecentres.pdf

Nunavut: http://www.gov.nu.ca/education/information/parents-young-children-0

POPULAR PLACES TO PUT YOUR CHILDCARE AD/ FIND CHILDCARE:

www.godaycare.com

www.daycarebear.com

www.care.com

www.canadiannanny.ca

www.nannycare.ca

Kijiji – but be careful!

Facebook childcare pages like KWC Childcare Providers and Parent Connect

Nanny Wage Calculator: https://www.care.com/en-ca/babysitting-rates

NANNY AGENCIES

www.nanniesoncall.com

http://nanniesinc.ca

Employment Contract Samples (includes Basic Contract, Medications Administration, Excursion form etc.)

Simply
Daycare: http://www.simplydaycare.com/home-daycare-forms.html

Care.com: https://www.care.com/homepay/
sample-nanny-contract-1309060137

Childcare Lounge: http://www.childcarelounge.com/
printables/printable-forms.php

Canadiannanny.ca: https://canadiannanny.ca/guide

VIDEOS:

canadiannanny.ca https://www.youtube.com/watch?v=FGhd6C0gEgI

Finding Quality
Childcare: http://findingqualitychildcare.ca/watch-the-vide

ERICK TRAPLIN

www.ericktraplin.com

Featured songs:

A Little More CD: A Little More

You're My Angel CD: A Little More

Bubbles CD: Bubbles

My Magic Carpet CD: My Magic Carpet

My Superhero CD: Bubbles

Questions: CD: Bubbles

Forever and a Day CD: My Magic Carpet

TOMORROW PHOTOGRAPHY

www.tomorrowphotography.com (Editor Jacki Lavigne's photography business)

FURTHER READING:

The Difference Between a Babysitter: 5 Myths Explained
by Ashley Books (I was interviewed for this article):
http://www.rasmussen.edu/degrees/education/blog
/difference-between-nanny-and-babysitter/

The New Family Project:
http://thenewfamily.com/2015/10/
1000-families-project-melissa-and-family/

Book: What to Expect the First Year By Heidi Murkoff

Book: The mother of all baby books: an all-Canadian guide to your baby's first year By: Ann Douglas

AFTERWARD

Throughout the duration of writing this book, I successfully helped two families acquire childcare through my contacts, advice, and list of questions to ask potential candidates. As well, I was inquired twice about myself being a family's nanny. I had to respectfully decline – Lauren still needs me full-time.

I really hope that this book has given you the tools to make the best informed childcare choice for your family. It may take a few or more candidates to find the best of the best childcare for your family. Look at me: in the 19 years as a Nanny, I had more than 16 interviews to land the seven chosen families I have cared for thus far. If you still need help, you can contact me at m.martz76@gmail.com

Now before I leave you, a word about the number 17. No, this is not a Sesame Street endorsement. I recently had to go to this particular street to drop off a book. I had been on this street before, but the house number didn't mean anything to me. Once I arrived at the house, it suddenly dawned on me that I had been interviewed at this house exactly three years ago to be the nanny at this house (different family). My current family's house number is 17, and look, even Mary Poppins resided with the Banks family at 17 Cherry Tree Lane.

So, if your house number is 17, and you are needing childcare for your child(ren); your choice might be right in front of you – a nanny.

Just sayin...

ACKNOWLEDGEMNETS

The saying *"no man is an island"* by poet John Drone or in this case, woman, is certainly true when you publish a book. It becomes more of *"it takes a village to publish a book"*.

I've been thinking about wriitng this book for quite awhile, and finally came into fruition. I have many people to thank for their insight, and their contributions to make this book a much needed guide to help parents acquire the best childcare for thier chidren.

Thank you to my editor and dear friend, Jacki Lavigne. You have worked tirelessly making sure the final draft was perfect. This is the second book you've edited for me, and you always do a top-notch job.

Thank you to my new friends at Tellwell Publishing in Victoria, BC; in particular Scott Lunn, Erin Ball and Liviu Peicu. I'm so glad I came across your website! From my initial contact to you inquire more information, I have been extremely impressed at how professional you are, and how much you care about us authors.

Thank you Erick Traplin for allowing me to print the lyrics to 'A Little More', 'You're My Angel', 'Bubbles', 'My Magic Carpet', 'My Super hero', 'Questions', and 'Forever and a Day'. Your unwavering friendship means so much to me.

Thank you Lisa Bendall for giving me permission to include 'Give Yourself a Break' and 'Gold Star Idea' from your book 'Raising a Kid with Special Needs'.

Thank you to everyone who contributed with an insight, interviews, and ideas. In particular, thank you goes out to: Heather, Denise, Jennifer 1, Jennifer 2, Ula, Tiffany, Tammy, Holly, Mariah, *Marcie, Susan, Kristen, *Karen, Jazmin, Cameron, Jenny, Kim, Leanne, Tanya, Bernie.